the power
of
DISCIPLING

GORDON FERGUSON

the power
of
DISCIPLING

DPI
DISCIPLESHIP
PUBLICATIONS
INTERNATIONAL

The Power of Discipling

© 2001 by Discipleship Publications International
2 Sterling Rd., Billerica, MA 01862-2595

Printed in the United States of America

ISBN: 1-57782-153-X

Cover Design: Tony Bonazzi
Interior Design: Corey Fisher

Contents

Publisher's Note

An emphasis on discipling relationships during the last thirty years of the twentieth century enabled God's people to grow and mature in some remarkable ways. A commitment to these Biblical relationships is crucial for the church to continue to fulfill its purpose. In 1997 DPI published *Discipling: God's Plan to Train and Transform His People*, a thorough treatment of this vital subject by Gordon Ferguson. More copies of that book have been sold than any other full-length book by an individual author ever published by DPI.

However, as new disciples continue to be added to God's kingdom, it was agreed that a shorter book which could be read more quickly was needed on the subject of discipling, to provide those new to the faith with a quicker way to grasp these vital principles. *The book you are holding does not contain any new material,* but is an abridged version of Gordon's earlier work. All of the chapters included here were found in the original work and have been condensed. The following chapters in the original have not been included here:

- A Theological Basis for Discipling Relationships
- Who Has Authority?
- The Challenge of Change
- Group Discipling
- Family Discipling

Those who finish this book and are looking for a more detailed discussion of various issues related to discipling relationships will find much helpful information in the original work which is still in print. It is the prayer of the author and the publisher that this important material presented in this new form will enable many new disciples to begin their life in Christ on firmer footing and with a greater vision of what God has in store.

part **one**

BIBLICAL FOUNDATIONS

chapter one

JESUS, THE MASTER DISCIPLER

If you have the world's most important message and you want to get it to the most people, how do you do it? Jesus had that conviction, and he had that concern. However, most Bible readers make some very erroneous assumptions about the ministry methods of Jesus. For years I was one of those people. I was very impressed with the times the Master Teacher worked with large crowds. I thought about how great it was for him to have exercised such magnetism that he was able to attract thousands at one time.

And yet, Jesus spoke to the crowds more as a means of training his apostles and other future evangelists (such as the seventy-two) than to "convert" the crowds. Of course, he was vitally interested in sharing God with those multitudes, but he wasn't naive enough to suppose that teaching in those large groups was going to really do the job of changing their lives. He realized that a more individualized approach was going to be necessary, and he was preparing some very special men to provide just that approach.

How We Learn Spiritual Truths

Most of what we learn in life is learned by OJT (on-the-job training). We watch big brother tie his shoes, and then we imitate him. We watch Dad change the tire on the car, and we quickly know far more than if we had spent a couple of hours reading the manual. Becoming a carpenter is a process: a journeyman repeatedly shows an apprentice how to do carpentry. Just about everything we learn in the early years of our lives is learned in this manner, as is most of what we learn in the later years. It is the fastest and easiest way and in many cases the only way to learn. Nowhere is this principle more important than in learning spiritual truths. Discipling, as we describe it in this book, is all about learning from someone else as they are following Jesus.

As we study the Scriptures, we see that there can be no "loner" Christians. We play an absolutely essential role in each other's lives. The gospel cannot be spread effectively without the human demonstration at the heart of it, nor can those who accept it be brought to maturity without those relationships (Matthew 28:19-20).

The Book alone is sufficient to reveal the content of the truth to man, but to grasp its power, we must read it both in black and white (pages) *and* in black, white, brown, red, and yellow (people). Can you see the point here? Discipleship has not been tried and found wanting; it has simply been found difficult and not often tried. However, when it is put into practice, lives change radically, and others are drawn to that magnet of visible change. Discipling works! And it is all that works! It was and is, without question, the plan of Jesus Christ for the salvation of the world.

The Plan of the Master

Years ago, when I was first learning about discipling, I read a very helpful little book entitled *The Master Plan of Evangelism.*[1] Coleman shows quite conclusively that the Master's method was men, plainly and simply. He poured his life into men, especially the Twelve, and when he returned to heaven, he left them to evangelize the world. They very effectively carried out his mission because they followed the same plan of pouring their lives into the lives of others, who repeated the same process over and over and over.

Christ's purpose was never to personally convert the masses, for in a physical body he was limited to one place at one time. However, through his spiritual body, the church, he could be everywhere at once. The masses are converted one by one. As I shared my faith yesterday with a young couple in a restaurant, disciples all over the world were doing the same. And as I slept last night, members of Jesus' body were carrying out his mission all over the world. Yes, the plan of Jesus was certainly the *master* plan!

The basics of his plan were as follows. First, he called men to follow him (Mark 1:14-18). Second, he kept men with him in order to train them and later send them out to share his message (Mark 3:14). Third, the training process included practical assignments, for we truly learn

[1] Robert E. Coleman, *The Master Plan of Evangelism* (Old Tappan, N.J.: Fleming H. Revell Company, 1963).

and retain only that which we practice. Finally, Jesus gave his life for what he had taught. Until we have something worth dying for, we have nothing worth living for.

After Jesus had been resurrected from the grave, he spent forty days preparing his trained men for the coming of the kingdom and the task of spreading it all over the world. He then ascended back to heaven, leaving these few ordinary men with the extraordinary task of *being* (not just preaching) Jesus to the world. As Paul put it in 2 Corinthians 5:20, "We are therefore Christ's ambassadors, as though God were making his appeal through us." Jesus' method was to pour his life into men, and once they were fully trained, they would be like him (Luke 6:40). Having been thus discipled, they were able to "go and make disciples of all nations, teaching them to obey everything I have commanded you" (Matthew 28:19-20). It was a simple plan with a high price tag of a tremendous personal investment in training individuals—but it worked. It remains the same simple plan, and the price tag is just as high. No other plan has ever worked, can ever work, will ever work. We either do it his way, or we fail miserably.

Jesus' Discipling Imitated

Jesus' apostles predictably followed the pattern they learned from him. After Philip had been with them, he was sent out to preach in Samaria, with great results (Acts 8). After Barnabas had been with them, he was sent to Antioch (Acts 11:22). He, in turn, went to find Saul (later known as Paul), a man of great potential, and discipled him in practical ministry. Jointly, they discipled many other leaders there in Antioch and, through the missionary journeys, made disciples and raised up leaders all over the world.

One of Paul's most influential disciples was Timothy. Their discipling relationship began when Timothy was a young disciple living in Lystra (Acts 16:1). Paul took him with him and Silas on the remainder of the second missionary tour for training and later sent him to lead the very prominent church in Ephesus. While there, Timothy received this very special charge about discipling from Paul: "And the things you have heard me say in the presence of many witnesses entrust to reliable men who will also be qualified to teach others" (2 Timothy 2:2). In chapter 3 we will examine this passage in more detail. Suffice it to say for now that establishing a *chain of discipling* is the intent of God in carrying out his mission on earth.

Paul had discipled Timothy, and Timothy was to disciple other reliable men, who would be able to teach others. Converting someone is never the ultimate goal of a disciple. The goal is to convert and train them to convert and train others, so that the chain will continue. In the case of Timothy, we have four spiritual generations implied in the above passage: Paul, Timothy, reliable men and others. When discipling is passed down through several generations, we can be assured that the discipleship concept is understood and will continue in the pattern Jesus envisioned.

Blessed Are My Eyes

God has allowed me to live to see these principles reinstated in a marvelous way. I am often reminded of these words of Jesus:

> "But blessed are your eyes because they see, and your ears because they hear. For I tell you the truth, many prophets and righteous men longed to see what you see but did not see it, and to hear what you hear but did not hear it."
> (Matthew 13:16-17)

After many years in the ministry, I had all but lost my dream of an evangelized world. I had nearly given up on finding a church in which total commitment was a standard rather than a mere ideal. Unfortunately, the constant disappointment and disillusionment of my years as a preacher had taken their toll on me spiritually, and my eyes were not blessed nearly as soon as they might have been.

However, by God's marvelous grace, I now hear stories of modern-day miracles practically daily, as lives are changed through the discipleship practiced all over the world, just as Jesus and the early church practiced it. Examples of multiplying disciplers in the Bible are wonderful to read about and learn from, but seeing present-day examples seems even more wonderful. Jesus is once again present in the flesh-and-blood examples of disciples making disciples who make disciples, in churches that multiply and send out, multiply and send out, as the world hears about our King Jesus, the Christ. His simple, yet highly effective, plan for conquering the world spiritually cannot be improved upon, and it is time that all who would follow him really start to follow his approach to discipleship. Praise God that we are out of the realms of theory and into the concrete examples of those who are doing it!

chapter two

DISCIPLING & ONE-ANOTHER RELATIONSHIPS

We have already seen that Jesus' plan to reach the world involved working through relationships. Now in this statement, we see that in unique relationships, Jesus' disciples would show the world the uniqueness of his work:

> "A new command I give you: Love one another. As I have loved you, so you must love one another. By this all men will know that you are my disciples, if you love one another." (John 13:34-35)

Everything Jesus taught was designed to create a church in which people would be faithful and helpful to one another in real life. The remainder of the New Testament shows that the apostles and others who penned the authoritative documents did not miss or misunderstand Jesus' message.

As you can see from the passages listed at the end of this chapter, the New Testament has a long list of directives about how those in the church are to relate to one another. All in all there are fifty-six verses with either "each other" or "one another" in them, and five of these verses have two such mentions, bringing the total to sixty-one. Life in the family of God is all about relationships—close, caring, responsive relationships. Some in the list tell us what we should be doing, and some tell us what to avoid. It is important to note that there are scores of other verses concerning relationships besides the ones that use this specific phraseology, but these fifty-six provide a fairly comprehensive description of godly relationships.

Even though the focus of this book is on discipling relationships, in one sense, *all* relationships in the body of Christ are to be "discipling" relationships. That is, in all our relationships, we are to be concerned with helping our brothers and sisters be faithful disciples of Jesus. However, we are talking here about a more specific relationship in which, for some period of time, one disciple makes a special commitment to the growth and encouragement of another disciple. As we look at the one-another commands, we would never argue that one-on-one discipling relationships are the *only* way to observe these instructions. Certainly, life in the body of Christ (what is often called "body life") in general must be based on them. None of these can be ignored in any spiritual relationship, but some of them are most readily put into practice in one-on-one discipling relationships.

Discipling has been rediscovered and reinstituted in modern times by those who have a passion to restore the relational nature of Biblical Christianity. They see how imperative it is that every church be a demonstration of these passages. They are right when they recognize that some one-another commands are easily omitted from our lives in the absence of best-friend discipling relationships.

For example, just think about how few church-goers confess their specific sins to another person (James 5:16). Think of those who never spiritually instruct other people (Romans 15:14) or admonish them (Colossians 3:16) or encourage them on a daily basis for the specific purpose of keeping their hearts soft and resistant to the hardening effects of sin (Hebrews 3:13). Oddly, many religious people have less than positive feelings about the discipleship-partner arrangement, yet their own lives are devoid of submission to many of these one-another commands. Whatever religious activities they may be involved in, they are not involved in the practice of these passages just mentioned. Such a lack of conviction and subsequent neglect surely must be seen by God as willful disobedience. Why would we find fault with anything that helps us more fully love, help, encourage and train one another?

Discipling and One-Another Passages

In the rest of this chapter we want to take just a few of these important one-another passages and look at how a special discipling relationship gives us a unique, but much needed, opportunity to put into practice the Biblical commands in a very consistent and life-changing fashion.

John 13:34-35—Love One Another

> "A new command I give you: Love *one another*. As I have loved you, so you must love *one*

> *another.* By this all men will know that you are
> my disciples, if you love *one another.*" (John
> 13:34-35, emphasis added)

As we mentioned earlier, the love demonstrated between disciples is to have a profound effect on the world who sees us together. Most often we think of assemblies of the body of Christ as the most appropriate way of making this demonstration. But this is not necessarily accurate. For example, in the Boston church of which I am a part, our assemblies make a powerful statement about race relationships. We have members who represent just about every race and combination of races possible. When nonmembers attend and see the hugs and warm greetings between races, it makes quite a powerful impression. Boston is characterized by its share of racial tensions, especially between blacks and whites, but the church strives mightily to be color blind. Therefore, attendance at our assemblies will allow visitors to experience the effects Jesus had in mind in John 13:34-35.

However, more impact is possible in smaller settings. Through a number of years, I have discipled brothers who are of different races than I am, including black, Hispanic and Asian (I'm white). Additionally, my wife and I have many close relationships in the kingdom with others from these backgrounds that we don't disciple directly. Our son's wife (to us, an adopted daughter by marriage, not a daughter-in-law!) is a delightful young Asian. With all of these, we are quite affectionate. Now don't you imagine that the impact of our relationship is more striking to onlookers than it would be in simply seeing us attend the same church? I think so. Some of my best spiritual friends are of different races than I, which makes some very strong statements to my neighbors, their neighbors and to all who see us together. While John 13:34-35 is fulfilled in many ways, to see best-friend discipleship partners loving as Jesus loved probably makes the point in the most dramatic fashion.

Hebrews 3:13—Encourage One Another Daily

> But encourage *one another* daily, as long as it is called Today, so that none of you may be hardened by sin's deceitfulness. (Hebrews 3:13, emphasis added)

Sin is deceitful. Our own sin deceives us into thinking we are doing better than we are, and we then proceed to deceive others around us into thinking we are doing better than we are. We are pretty clueless about the lives of the people we see only in larger church settings. We have to know people well to know how they are doing spiritually and to be able to tell when they are becoming blind or hardened to their own spiritual condition.

Certain people cannot be fooled. Wives are not oblivious to their husband's spirituality level. After thirty-two years of marriage, I sometimes think that Theresa knows me better than I know myself, and quite often she does. I desperately need her input, because she loves me most and knows me best.

Discipleship partners develop the same types of insight into our spiritual lives, because they are around us a lot and know us. Our relationship is to be based on honesty and vulnerability. We all need people in our lives who know us and love us enough to help us when we are veering off the narrow path. Even when we are mostly deceived by and about our sins, we sense that something is unsettled in our souls. Then when our discipleship partner says, "How are you doing?" we might answer quickly, "Fine," but if he (or she, if you are a woman) knows us well, he won't leave the issue too quickly. The next question is often, "How are you *really* doing?" At that point we start getting in touch and being real. For me, if I truly don't know what is wrong with me, talking with my discipler usually drives the issue to the surface, and I am on my way back to an even keel.

Of course, then, in Hebrews 3:13, we have to deal with the "daily" encouragement issue. The passage does not say we must have a daily relationship with any one person, but if that has been found to be a great help to disciples, why would we not be eager to have it? Given the busyness of many of our lives, keeping in touch with each other daily can be a challenge. We need to see it, however, not as a legalistic requirement, but as a great opportunity to stay in step with the Spirit.

Hebrews 10:24—Spur One Another On

> And let us consider how we may spur *one another* on toward love and good deeds. (Hebrews 10:24, emphasis added)

Now this is an intriguing passage. The original Greek word translated "spur on" *(paroxysmos)* has an interesting history. It has a very definite connection with anger. At best, the word carries the idea of being very passionate about something to the point that becoming heated about it would be a natural response. It was not a word used for conflict avoiders and people pleasers. We find it twice in the New Testament: once in this passage and once in Acts 15:39. In the latter it is translated "sharp disagreement," as it describes an encounter between Paul and Barnabas when they were discussing the role of John Mark in their mission efforts. The disagreement was so sharp that these two great missionaries parted company!

Hebrews 10:24 is saying that another's spiritual life is worth fighting for, if need be. Surely this is the language of relationships, close relationships. Barnabas discipled Paul in the early stages of their relationship, and Paul loved and respected Barnabas immensely. They were secure enough in their love to lay all of their cards on the table. All indications are that they kept the highest regard for one another, even after their disagreement. Interestingly, near the end of his life Paul requested Mark's help in his ministry (2 Timothy 4:11). With whom do you have this kind of relationship? The person you only greet in the foyer before or after a church service? No, we must have close relationships for these kinds of potentially heated interactions, and no relationship lends itself to it more than a discipling relationship.

James 5:16—Confess to One Another

> Therefore confess your sins to *each other* and
> pray for *each other* so that you may be healed.
> The prayer of a righteous man is powerful and
> effective. (James 5:16, emphasis added)

Confession of sins is vital if we are to overcome Satan's power in our lives. He is a creature of darkness, and thrives well only in his native environment. If we get ourselves out into the light, he runs. James promised in James 4:7 that if we resist Satan, he will flee from us. But how do we resist him? With light. The more light, the more he is rendered powerless. The Bible is light, and studying it definitely limits Satan. Spiritual activities and spiritual relationships limit him. The closer we are to God, the less the devil can do to hurt us. The more we surround ourselves with spiritual things, the less he can get a foothold in our hearts.

What is hidden inside us remains in the darkness. Only by getting it out and exposing it to other people do we ourselves see it clearly. When we confess sin, the light destroys sin's grip. The world has this concept exactly backwards, which is not surprising. Confessing one's sins is considered lunacy by most. So they keep sin hidden in darkness, and its effects multiply mightily. Read John 3:19-21 in this vein, and ask yourself whether you love coming out into the light or staying hidden in darkness.

The grammatical construction of the Greek in James 5:16 shows the need for a habitual, continual confessing of sins. "Be in the habit of confessing" is the idea. It is also important to note that we are to confess specific sins, not just that we have sinned. The more specific, the more light and the more victory we can have over them. Years ago when the magnitude of this principle dawned on me, I came up with a plan to defeat the sins in my life. First, I would confess very specifically and graphically to God, to the point of embarrassment. This in itself introduces copious amounts of light onto the situation. Then I would confess to a brother. If no victory came at that point, then I made my confession to a *group* of men. I determined to confess to larger and larger groups until the light blinded Satan and ran him off (at least on that point). The first time I tried it in those years before I was a part of a discipling ministry, I ended up going all the way to the whole congregation with the confession. As my face blushed with embarrassment, Satan cowered with light overdose and left me alone! The practice works if we have the conviction to work it.

But one more word on confessing specifically. While preaching, I often use stories from my own life because I want to model openness for others, and I want the benefit of throwing the light in Satan's eyes. Mentioning in a general way that I struggle with lust is not out of place in a congregational setting. But mentioning the specifics of it would be. Yet, if I am to have a victory, I need to confess the specifics. To whom should I confess? To Theresa? Probably not. My own opinion on this sensitive area is that wives don't quite understand men's struggles in this regard, because for women lust typically involves more of an emotional attraction. Therefore, they may assume that we are emotionally attracted to someone when we are not, and this assumption can affect them detrimentally.

My discipleship partner is the ideal one with whom to share my inmost struggles. If you are a man, he is a man and understands what you are going through and can help you. In this illustration, the wife would be protected and the man helped by specific confession. The only exception I normally make in this approach is to recommend a brother confessing to his wife if other measures don't produce repentance. For example, I have known of men who needed to confess to their wives repeated late-night channel surfing on TV and using the computer to view pornography on the Internet. Confession to the wife would certainly increase the wattage of the light exposure! (And it normally works wonders in inducing repentance!) We need to have a natural avenue of confessing all temptations and sins. The sensitivity of the area mentioned above shows the need for and the wisdom of having these close, one-on-one relationships between those whom we call discipleship partners.

Ephesians 5:21—Submit to One Another

> Submit to *one another* out of reverence for Christ. (Ephesians 5:21, emphasis added)

Mutual submission is part of the foundation of spiritual relationships between all brothers and sisters in Christ.

Nevertheless, Paul reiterates this command for mutual submission before addressing the husband/wife relationship. He may have done so to tie this passage in with the earlier part of the chapter; indeed, the command fits all relationships in some way. In the marriage relationship, wives are to submit to the *leadership* of their husbands, and husbands are to submit to the *needs* of their wives by loving them as Christ loves the church. (Modern society may take offense at God's teachings, but God takes offense at their teachings and the divorce rate they produce!)

Submission comes in many forms, as leadership and followership are part of all our lives. In some areas I lead, and I expect others involved in those areas to submit to my leadership. In other areas I am led, and I willingly submit to those leading me in those areas. For example, Randy McKean is my lead evangelist, and I submit to him in that role. I am his teacher, and he submits to me in that role (and does quite well on ministry training exams, I might add!). Submission is a part of orderly life, and the less of it any society, group or family has, the more chaos will reign.

But what does all of this have to do with discipling? Let's appeal to the same logic we used with the commands we have already discussed. Submission to one another is quite vaguely expressed in a large-group setting, except for the role of the leaders and those under them. It comes into play between "one another" at the more intimate levels of relationship. Certainly the discipleship-partner relationships require this kind of submissive heart. We cannot be discipled without a willingness to be discipled, and that certainly involves some type of submission. (In the later chapters of *Discipling: God's Plan to Train and Transform His People* I clarify some related issues regarding differences in spiritual maturity, age or experience that exist between discipleship partners.)

I was discipled for a few years by Jimmy Rogers, who is nearly fifteen years younger than I. Once in a sermon, he mentioned that discipling me was a major two-lane road. In other words, the discipling went both ways. Actually, it should always go both ways to some extent (unless, of course, one of the discipleship partners is Jesus!). Jimmy and I are both in the leadership group of the Boston church, and we both wear many hats of leadership. But back then I still strove to have a submissive spirit toward Jimmy and looked at him as a tool of God in helping me grow.

Authority and submission are most often viewed negatively. However, we must learn to see them Biblically as very positive. I deeply appreciate those in the kingdom of God who will accept leadership roles because I know that Jesus demands that his leaders be servants—submissive to the needs of those they lead. I am grateful to submit to godly leadership. I am grateful for those "willing volunteers" (Judges 5:9) who submit to my leadership. Our submission in discipling relationships is not really submission to the *authority* of the discipler; it is submission to the authority of God, who has chosen to work in our lives through human tools.

Romans 15:14—Instruct One Another

> I myself am convinced, my brothers, that you
> yourselves are full of goodness, complete in
> knowledge and competent to instruct *one
> another.* (Romans 15:14, emphasis added)

Competency to instruct one another, according to this passage, is based on two things: being filled with goodness and being complete in knowledge. Just what does being "complete in knowledge" entail? Certainly it would include a knowledge of the word of God. We cannot instruct, counsel or advise without a basic understanding of the Biblical issues involved in helping one another spiritually. But this knowledge would necessarily include our familiarity with the person we are trying to help. *Those who know me best are able to help me most.*

In a men's discipleship group of eight leaders, we spent some time talking about our personal spiritual lives. This was followed by a brief evaluation of each person by others in the group who noted one strength and one area most needing improvement. Randy McKean, who was leading the group, asked us to share only about the person sitting to our right. Although that method of selection was purely arbitrary, I was glad that I was sitting to the right of Randy, since he disciples me at this point in my life and knows me better than some others in the group know me. He picked the weak point I most needed to hear at that time (although others could have been selected!).

Later that night, as Theresa and I were driving home from our discipleship groups, I shared with her the gist of Randy's comments. She became quiet, and after about a minute I looked over at her and noticed that she was crying. My first thought (obviously an *unspiritual* one!) was that she felt defensive for me! That was hardly the case. Upon hearing about Randy's critique, she started getting in touch with some emotions that totally validated the critique. In a word, the sinful tendency which had been pointed out in me (essentially, impatience and irritability) was the very sin which had hurt her. We spent several hours talking that night and on the following day. She was able to have her heart healed and her husband repentant. The level of conviction produced in me has enabled me to make some great strides, thank God, but the beginning point was that d-group.

Ephesians 4:32—Forgive One Another

> Be kind and compassionate to *one another*, forgiving *each other*, just as in Christ God forgave you. (Ephesians 4:32, emphasis added)

Forgiveness is a wonderful, godly quality, but its presence is needed only when ungodly qualities have entered the scene! Sin must occur before forgiveness is needed. Now, against whom do you most sin—those you are around most or least? Those who see me only in a larger church setting often seem to think I am *Mr. Wonderful* and *Mr. Perfect*. Why is that? I often mention in lessons that I am far from perfect and share instances in my life (like the one above) to demonstrate it. But most of the people in the audience are not in my life at the more intimate levels, and we don't have many opportunities to sin against each other. Those who are in my life at the closer levels see and are hurt by my sins more readily; and since they have more expectations in our relationship, they are more prone to be hurt by me.

Therefore, although forgiveness is vital in all relationships when sin occurs, the fact remains that relationship sins occur most in the closest relationships. I'm reminded of an old song with this line in it: "You always hurt the one you love." (No surprises there—they are about the only ones who will put up with you long enough to get hurt by you!) And the more love there is, the deeper the hurt can be. You could never wound a casual friend as deeply as you can an intimate friend. I am persuaded that Ephesians 4:32 is needed and exercised most in the relationships which are the closest to us.

Philippians 4:2—Agree with One Another

> I plead with Euodia and I plead with Syntyche to agree with *each other* in the Lord. (Philippians 4:2, emphasis added)

Agreement with each other, in the case of Euodia and Syntyche, was needed due to some disagreement between them which had affected the church. We have to assume that these women were key leaders, or else Paul would not have mentioned their names publicly. They, in fact, had been co-workers with him when he had been in Philippi, according to Philippians 4:3. Such disagreements could only occur between those with a close relationship. Whether they were what we are terming "discipleship partners" or not, they must have been functioning in a similar manner. We generally do not have disagreements like this one without first having a close working relationship.

Some time ago, I was speaking with a brother about a disagreement he had experienced in the past. He felt badly about the disagreement (which, in this case, involved some incorrect assumptions), but I was not alarmed by it, especially since he and the brother had worked it out. My comment to him was that disagreements, when resolved correctly, bind us closer together. My closest relationships are those in which some rather heated disagreements have occurred and been resolved.

When we first moved to Boston and Wyndham Shaw was discipling me, I was unsatisfied with only one thing in our otherwise good relationship. I was quite open with him about my life (including my sins), but he didn't reciprocate. Once I asked if we could take a long walk together around a lake, and during the walk, I expressed my disagreement with his approach on this one point. My ultimate issue was that no relationship can ever be really close without both people being vulnerable. He began the conversation disagreeing with me, saying that he was open with his discipler, just as I was with him, and that was sufficient. He said that what we really needed to get closer

was to get more time playing sports together! Our disagreement continued for most of our walk around the
lake. After some fairly intense exchanges, he changed his
mind. He then changed his practice immediately, and by
example, called me higher in that very area! We were more
bonded that day through our frank disagreement and resolution than we would have been after ten days on the
basketball court!

While discipleship partner relationships are not the
only way to put into practice these vital one-another passages, they are often the best. And without such relationships, my experience is that some of the passages will be
seldom practiced, if ever. We all need each other in the
church, every member, for we are a family. But as in a
physical family, we need that special one with whom we
can pour out our hearts freely in a confidential setting,
who will be able to help our heart and its problems
because of the closeness of the relationship. I thank God
for discipling relationships!

New Testament One-Another Passages

1. *Mark 9:50*—Salt is good, but if it loses its saltiness, how can you make it salty again? Have salt in yourselves, and be at peace with *each other.*

2. *John 13:34*—A new command I give you: Love *one another.* As I have loved you, so you must love *one another.*

3. *John 13:35*—By this all men will know that you are my disciples, if you love *one another.*

4. *John 15:12*—My command is this: Love *each other* as I have loved you.

5. *John 15:17*—This is my command: Love *each other.*

6. *Romans 12:10*—Be devoted to *one another* in brotherly love. Honor *one another* above yourselves.

7. *Romans 12:16*—Live in harmony with *one another.* Do not be proud, but be willing to associate with people of low position. Do not be conceited.

8. *Romans 13:8*—Let no debt remain outstanding, except the continuing debt to love *one another,* for he who loves his fellowman has fulfilled the law.

9. *Romans 14:13*—Therefore let us stop passing judgment on *one another.* Instead, make up your mind not to put any stumbling block or obstacle in your brother's way.

10. *Romans 15:7*—Accept *one another*, then, just as Christ accepted you, in order to bring praise to God.

11. *Romans 15:14*—I myself am convinced, my brothers, that you yourselves are full of goodness, complete in knowledge and competent to instruct *one another.*

12. *Romans 16:16*—Greet *one another* with a holy kiss. All the churches of Christ send greetings.

13. *1 Corinthians 1:10*—I appeal to you, brothers, in the name of our Lord Jesus Christ, that all of you agree with *one another* so that there may be no divisions among you and that you may be perfectly united in mind and thought.

14. *1 Corinthians 7:5*—Do not deprive *each other* except by mutual consent and for a time, so that you may devote yourselves to prayer. Then come together again so that Satan will not tempt you because of your lack of self-control.

15. *1 Corinthians 11:33*—So then, my brothers, when you come together to eat, wait for *each other.*

16. *1 Corinthians 12:25*— . . . so that there should be no division in the body, but that its parts should have equal concern for *each other.*

17. *1 Corinthians 16:20*—All the brothers here send you greetings. Greet *one another* with a holy kiss.

18. *2 Corinthians 13:12*—Greet *one another* with a holy kiss.

19. *Galatians 5:13*—You, my brothers, were called to be free. But do not use your freedom to indulge the sinful nature; rather, serve *one another* in love.

20. *Galatians 5:15*—If you keep on biting and devouring *each other*, watch out or you will be destroyed by *each other.*

21. *Galatians 5:26*—Let us not become conceited, provoking and envying *each other.*

22. *Ephesians 4:2*—Be completely humble and gentle; be patient, bearing with *one another* in love.

23. *Ephesians 4:32*—Be kind and compassionate to one another, forgiving *each other*, just as in Christ God forgave you.

24. *Ephesians 5:19*—Speak to *one another* with psalms, hymns and spiritual songs. Sing and make music in your heart to the Lord,

25. *Ephesians 5:21*—Submit to *one another* out of reverence for Christ.

26. *Philippians 4:2*—I plead with Euodia and I plead with Syntyche to agree with *each other* in the Lord.

27. *Colossians 3:9*—Do not lie to *each other,* since you have taken off your old self with its practices

28. *Colossians 3:13*—Bear with *each other* and forgive whatever grievances you may have against *one another.* Forgive as the Lord forgave you.

29. *Colossians 3:16*—Let the word of Christ dwell in you richly as you teach and admonish *one another* with all wisdom, and as you sing psalms, hymns and spiritual songs with gratitude in your hearts to God.

30. *1 Thessalonians 3:12*—May the Lord make your love increase and overflow for *each other* and for everyone else, just as ours does for you.

31. *1 Thessalonians 4:9*—Now about brotherly love we do not need to write to you, for you yourselves have been taught by God to love *each other.*

32. *1 Thessalonians 4:18*—Therefore encourage *each other* with these words.

33. *1 Thessalonians 5:11*—Therefore encourage *one another* and build *each other* up, just as in fact you are doing.

34. *1 Thessalonians 5:13*—Hold them in the highest regard in love because of their work. Live in peace with *each other*.

35. *1 Thessalonians 5:15*—Make sure that nobody pays back wrong for wrong, but always try to be kind to *each other* and to everyone else.

36. *2 Thessalonians 1:3*—We ought always to thank God for you, brothers, and rightly so, because your faith is growing more and more, and the love every one of you has for *each other* is increasing.

37. *Hebrews 3:13*—But encourage *one another* daily, as long as it is called Today, so that none of you may be hardened by sin's deceitfulness.

38. *Hebrews 10:24*—And let us consider how we may spur *one another* on toward love and good deeds.

39. *Hebrews 10:25*—Let us not give up meeting together, as some are in the habit of doing, but let us encourage *one another*—and all the more as you see the Day approaching.

40. *Hebrews 13:1*—Keep on loving *each other* as brothers.

41. *James 4:11*—Brothers, do not slander *one another*. Anyone who speaks against his brother or judges him speaks against the law and judges it. When you judge the law, you are not keeping it, but sitting in judgment on it.

42. *James 5:9*—Don't grumble against *each other,* brothers, or you will be judged. The Judge is standing at the door!

43. *James 5:16*—Therefore confess your sins to *each other* and pray for *each other* so that you may be healed. The prayer of a righteous man is powerful and effective.

44. *1 Peter 1:22*—Now that you have purified yourselves by obeying the truth so that you have sincere love for your brothers, love *one another* deeply, from the heart.

45. *1 Peter 3:8*—Finally, all of you, live in harmony with *one another;* be sympathetic, love as brothers, be compassionate and humble.

46. *1 Peter 4:8*—Above all, love *each other* deeply, because love covers over a multitude of sins.

47. *1 Peter 4:9*—Offer hospitality to *one another* without grumbling.

48. *1 Peter 5:5*—Young men, in the same way be submissive to those who are older. All of you, clothe yourselves with humility toward *one another,* because, "God opposes the proud but gives grace to the humble."

49. *1 Peter 5:14*—Greet *one another* with a kiss of love. Peace to all of you who are in Christ.

50. *1 John 1:7*—But if we walk in the light, as he is in the light, we have fellowship with *one another*, and the blood of Jesus, his Son, purifies us from all sin.

51. *1 John 3:11*—This is the message you heard from the beginning: We should love *one another.*

52. *1 John 3:23*—And this is his command: to believe in the name of his Son, Jesus Christ, and to love *one another* as he commanded us.

53. *1 John 4:7*—Dear friends, let us love *one another*, for love comes from God. Everyone who loves has been born of God and knows God.

54. *1 John 4:11*—Dear friends, since God so loved us, we also ought to love *one another*.

55. *1 John 4:12*—No one has ever seen God; but if we love *one another*, God lives in us and his love is made complete in us.

56. *2 John 1:5*—And now, dear lady, I am not writing you a new command but one we have had from the beginning. I ask that we love *one another*.

chapter three

BIBLICAL PRINCIPLES OF DISCIPLING

Biblical discipling is a good idea, but it is more than that. I believe we will see in this chapter that discipling is a matter of absolute necessity for anyone who would take seriously the teaching of the New Testament. We will examine Biblical passages which show the basis of having such relationships and provide the directions for gaining the most benefit from them.

The first murder in the world was committed because of the breakdown of brotherly relationships. When God asked Cain about his brother Abel, Cain replied, "Am I my brother's keeper?" (Genesis 4:9). The remainder of the Bible shouts, "Yes!" Of the thousands of truths taught in the Bible, none is clearer than the fact that we emphatically are to be our brother's keeper. The greatest command in all of Scripture is to love God with our entire being and to love our neighbors as ourselves (Matthew 22:36-40). Must we love our spiritual brothers? Absolutely! But how does that love show itself? In myriad ways, but one of the most important is to love enough to help each other grow and change to be more like Christ.

Discipleship demands that we put our laziness behind us and serve another for his highest good. It demands that we put off our pride and humbly submit to the leadership of others and to the needs of others. It demands that we put aside our people-pleasing, conflict-avoiding natures and reach out to those who need our direction and correction. It demands that we follow the One who set the pattern for it and died for it and spelled it out in his word for us. Are we willing? Since "faith comes from hearing the message, and the message is heard through the word of Christ" (Romans 10:17), let's go to that message and deepen our convictions about discipling relationships.

Old Testament Principles

Many passages show the value of close relationships which challenge us to be our best for God. At a later time, we will mention a number of scriptures, particularly in Proverbs, that talk about seeking advice and responding wisely to correction. Characteristic of such verses are these: "Whoever loves discipline loves knowledge, but he who hates correction is stupid" (Proverbs 12:1) and "Listen to advice and accept instruction, and in the end you will be wise" (Proverbs 19:20). These are general discipleship verses, for they show the importance of having others in our lives to advise, instruct and correct us.

The most classic passages in Proverbs on the subject are in chapter 27:

> Better is open rebuke
> than hidden love.

Wounds from a friend can be trusted,
   but an enemy multiplies kisses. (27:5-6)

As iron sharpens iron,
   so one man sharpens another. (27:17)

Such verses presuppose really close relationships that call out the best in each other. I don't particularly *enjoy* open rebuke, but I have grown to *appreciate* it. Some of the most valuable lessons in my life have come from the mouth of someone willing to lay out the truth to me. I neither enjoy nor appreciate hidden love or hidden displeasure or any other hidden agenda. Bottom line, I appreciate honesty. Whatever you are really thinking about me, just come out with it! Real relationships are just that—real (open and honest).

I remember a time when my daughter, Renee, was a teen, and we were having difficulties in our relationship, and we needed help. Randy McKean suggested that he come over so he could disciple us both together. I asked Renee how she felt about going this route, and she said, "Fine, because I know you will get yours too!" Randy was evenhanded, and sure enough, we both got ours. Afterward, Randy asked if he had been too hard on me (not wanting to show disrespect to me as an older man). I told him that he had been very honest and straightforward, but impartial, in his correction. I expected nothing less and would not have been satisfied with anything less.

But be prepared: When iron sharpens iron, some sparks are going to fly. I have forgotten thousands of pleasant conversations through the years, but I have some heated conversations firmly etched in my memory. They may have seemed tough at the moment, but the closest relationships have been forged at the fire of tension and the anvil of resolution. Let's develop the heart of the psalmist when he wrote:

> Let a righteous man strike me—it is a kindness;
>> let him rebuke me—it is oil on my head.
> My head will not refuse it. (Psalm 141:5)

A passage seldom used in this context, but one which is nonetheless full of discipling principles is Ecclesiastes 4:8-12.

> There was a man all alone;
>> he had neither son nor brother.
> There was no end to his toil,
>> yet his eyes were not content with his
>> wealth.
> "For whom am I toiling," he asked,
>> "and why am I depriving myself of
>> enjoyment?"
> This too is meaningless—
>> a miserable business!
>
> Two are better than one,
>> because they have a good return for their
>> work:

If one falls down,
>   his friend can help him up.
But pity the man who falls
>   and has no one to help him up!
Also, if two lie down together, they will keep
>   warm.
>   But how can one keep warm alone?
Though one may be overpowered,
>   two can defend themselves.
A cord of three strands is not quickly broken.

This passage is often applied to marriage and is thus used as a part of wedding ceremonies. We can certainly make such an application, but in context, it is simply describing the need we all have for close relationships. Take a closer look at the wording of the passage. A man alone, without family or close friend will never be satisfied with a career and wealth (v8). Life is about relationships, not possessions or accomplishments. We need a buddy to help us work and to help us up when we fall. Teamwork not only increases accomplishment, it makes work much more enjoyable. Who helps the average person get up when he falls?

Years ago, I remember facing some personal struggles of a fairly ordinary nature. I had no one with whom I talked about such things, but I dared venture out to talk with a good fishing buddy. After pouring out my pain, he just looked at me and said, "Oh." No more, no less—just, "Oh." You can bet that I didn't try that openness stuff again for a long time! Certainly not until I found the kind of friend described in the above passage—namely a spiritual friend. In verse 12, "the cord of three strands" may simply refer to three close friends, teaching that if a relationship of two is helpful, then three together is even better. Peter, James and John would agree with that one! A deeper meaning may be that two spiritual friends bound to God are unstoppable. I like that idea better, though I am not sure that the writer had it in mind.

While the Old Testament taught in principle the need for close relationships designed to call each other higher, the New Testament teaches this much more directly. Let's take a look at some of the key passages in it.

Key New Testament Passages

The Commission

Although I believe many, many passages show the need for discipling relationships, Matthew 28:19-20 is, in some ways, the clearest.

> "Therefore go and make disciples of all nations, baptizing them in the name of the Father and of the Son and of the Holy Spirit, and teaching them to obey everything I have commanded you. And surely I am with you always, to the very end of the age."

Several foundational lessons are contained in this passage. First, we are to make disciples—not simply church members, religious people or nicer humans. This means that before any person is a Biblical candidate for baptism, he must have made the *decision* to be a disciple (and he must have learned enough of what this means to make an educated decision).

Second, Matthew 28 teaches that we are to baptize them. This would have to be with the one baptism of Ephesians 4:5. This baptism in *form* is a burial in water (Acts 8:34-39, Romans 6:3-4). It, in *intent*, is a decision to be a disciple in all of the ways described in the New Testament. It should be rather obvious that no one can be Biblically baptized until they are old enough to make such a decision and then follow through with it. Choosing to be a disciple is just that: a choice.

Third, the passage shows that we are to teach them (the baptized ones) to obey everything that Jesus commanded the apostles. Just like every child born into a family has to be trained, every child in God's family must be trained. We are not simply to *teach* everything Jesus commanded, but to teach to obey.

I remember my experience of planning the curriculum for the traditional churches of which I was a part. We had our five-year plans for teaching through the Bible, but I assure you that we never had any intentions of teaching the members to *obey!* They had not made a disciple's commitment, and they were not about to have anyone disturb their complacency. Had anyone come close to *insisting* on obedience to everything Christ taught, we would have lost members quickly!

But we need to examine this passage more closely, especially verse 20 and its directive to teach disciples to obey everything that Jesus taught. What is the most effective way to teach a person initially to come to Christ—in a group or as an individual? Obviously, the smaller the setting, the more personalized the teaching. Agreed?

After baptism, what is the most effective way to train them to obey everything—in an assembly of hundreds or in an individual manner? Isn't the answer obvious? I'm reminded of the person who heard about discipling relationships and commented, "Well, that may sound good to some, but how do you square it with the Biblical teaching about personal privacy?" Well as far as I can tell, that teaching simply does not exist in the Bible, but when my children were young and didn't want their parents in their lives training them, I'm sure they wished that it did! However, it was not a part of my parental doctrine, because I was intent on training my children to be responsible, righteous adults. Nor is it a part of God's doctrine, for he is intent on all disciples being trained, and therefore all who are a part of his family are responsible for each other's spiritual well-being and growth.

I have yet to see how Jesus' commands in Matthew 28 can be carried out except when someone is directly responsible for the training in every disciple's life. Just attending church could not possibly accomplish what is being commanded, for it takes a specific person to train another specific person in the specific commands of Jesus.

The Leadership Provision

Leadership has been planned and provided by God to ensure that his mission for the church is accomplished.

It was he who gave some to be apostles, some to be prophets, some to be evangelists, and some to be pastors and teachers, to prepare God's people for works of service, so that the body of Christ may be built up until we all reach unity in the faith and in the knowledge of the Son of God and become mature, attaining to the whole measure of the fullness of Christ.

Then we will no longer be infants, tossed back and forth by the waves, and blown here and there by every wind of teaching and by the cunning and craftiness of men in their deceitful scheming. Instead, speaking the truth in love, we will in all things grow up into him who is the Head, that is, Christ. From him the whole body, joined and held together by every supporting ligament, grows and builds itself up in love, as each part does its work. (Ephesians 4:11-16)

These few verses encapsulate most of what has already been said about discipleship and the role it must play in God's kingdom. Leaders are to prepare God's people for works of service ("works of ministry"—RSV), not do the work for them! The goal of this training is for the church to be built up in unity and knowledge, becoming like Christ. When the church is matured into the fullness of Christ, the onlooking world can be attracted through us to him. We must note the emphasis on every disciple being trained. Such maturity comes only when all disciples are fully trained to obey all that Jesus commanded, just as he taught in Matthew 28. The unity necessary for effective evangelism (John 13 and 17) comes when leaders train disciples as Jesus did. Then the church grows because every part does its work, with Jesus himself being the standard for every person's spiritual life—nothing less will do.

The idea of leaders raising up a united body of believers, mature in love and knowledge, spreading the gospel through teaching and living the gospel is thought to be impossible. And it *is* impossible without discipling, God's process of training and maturing disciples. However, when leaders are personally involved in training others to personally train others, amazing things happen. The next passage shows how this works.

The Discipling Chain

Paul gave very specific and practical advice to his own young disciple in 2 Timothy 2:1-7:

> You then, my son, be strong in the grace that is in Christ Jesus. And the things you have heard me say in the presence of many witnesses entrust to reliable men who will also be qualified to teach others. Endure hardship with us like a good soldier of Christ Jesus. No one serving as a soldier gets involved in civilian affairs—he wants to please his commanding officer.

> Similarly, if anyone competes as an athlete, he
> does not receive the victor's crown unless he
> competes according to the rules. The hard-
> working farmer should be the first to receive a
> share of the crops. Reflect on what I am saying,
> for the Lord will give you insight into all this.

This text not only outlines the process of establishing a chain of discipling relationships, but it also describes the qualities demanded of both the discipler and the disciple in order to make the chain function effectively. (We will reserve comment on most of these qualities until later chapters, since these considerations fit more naturally into those discussions.) Paul does provide some great insights into the discipling process, although he informs us that we will have to open our hearts to it by doing some reflection on it (v7).

Paul had committed everything he knew about the heart and soul of ministry to Timothy, and now he asks Timothy to pass these things on to reliable men. "Reliable" men (or "faithful"—KJV) were to be Timothy's focus. Paul and Timothy were following Jesus' example of focusing his efforts on fully training a few in order to not dilute his long-term impact. No one—not even Jesus—can fully equip the multitudes, and thus choices must be made. Leaders today need to ask themselves, "Who can I best train to affect the most other people for Christ in the most dramatic fashion?" Timothy undoubtedly had to determine how many men he could effectively disciple, and then which were the most reliable (or "faithful"—"full of faith"). The things Timothy had heard from Paul were not abstract theological precepts; they were issues involving the lifestyle of disciples who were imitating Jesus.

When Timothy received his letters of instruction, he was leading the church in Ephesus. Since Paul had established the church there, Timothy was well aware of how the church had been led by Paul, and he was intent on imitating his leadership. In Acts 20:17-38, Paul recounted his days in Ephesus. They were characterized by his teaching publicly and from house to house (large settings and small). As he lived among them, he warned them and pleaded with them to live the life of disciples. He worked hard, pouring out his life for them and into them. And he put his whole heart into it, which was shown by his mention twice of serving them "with tears." Discipling other people is no easy matter! It isn't possible unless we make a disciple's commitment to Jesus, for the sacrifice is great. But the cause is the most important on planet Earth, and it cannot be successful without the entrusting of our hearts and lives to others.

The Commitment to Perfection

Our final passage to examine in this chapter is Colossians 1:27-29:

> To them God has chosen to make known among the Gentiles the glorious riches of this

Kingdom Media Resources

655 W. Grand Ave Suite 220
Elmhurst, IL 60126
630-279-3645 x311

A Ministry of the Chicago Church of Christ

_A/_	_11/18_	_Sgr_
Region	Date	Seller

Purchaser

Qty	KMR Item Number	Each	Total
2	5395	650	13 00

Cash	(Check)		Total	13 00
Master Card	Visa		Shipping	
Discover	AMEX		**Grand Total**	13 00

ver 1.6 6/8/01

> mystery, which is Christ in you, the hope of
> glory.
>
> We proclaim him, admonishing and teach-
> ing everyone with all wisdom, so that we may
> present everyone perfect in Christ. To this end
> I labor, struggling with all his energy, which so
> powerfully works in me.

These verses reiterate the extent of dedication needed to disciple others to maturity in Christ. Paul said that he taught, proclaimed and admonished everyone with his God-given wisdom. His goal was to present every disciple perfect ("mature" in the RSV) in Christ. Only when this maturity is our goal can the fullness of Jesus be seen in us (Colossians 1:27); only when this fullness is seen will the world be attracted to him; and this fullness is only possible with the kind of focused discipling mentioned in this passage. Regardless of which passage about discipleship we read, the same points are made, emphasized and implied.

What kind of discipling is taught by Paul here? It is a purposeful kind: "to this end," meaning the maturity in Christ we are to attain, making "Christ in us" a reality. It is a sacrificial kind, requiring "labor" (literally "toil which exhausts"), "struggling" and "energy" which only God can supply. Paul further describes this strenuous type of discipling in this way:

> I want you to know how much I am struggling
> for you and for those at Laodicea, and for all

> who have not met me personally. My purpose
> is that they may be encouraged in heart and
> united in love, so that they may have the full
> riches of complete understanding, in order that
> they may know the mystery of God, namely,
> Christ. (Colossians 2:1-2)

Why did he want them to know how great a struggle it was discipling others to Christ? Because they all were to imitate it (see 1 Corinthians 4:16, 11:1).

Paul does not mention the discipling-chain process here, but it was definitely involved. Neither he nor any other person, including Jesus, could present the masses perfect in Christ. He could work closely with kingdom leaders like Timothy and Titus and pour his heart into them. They in turn could pour their lives into others under their leadership, who could do the same with yet others, and on and on until every person could be matured in Christ. When a discipling passage does not specifically mention this chain process, we must conclude that it is presupposed because (1) it was evident in the lives of Jesus and the apostles and (2) common sense tells us no other method would have worked. The world cannot be reached unless the church is matured enough to demonstrate Jesus' fullness to them, thus attracting them to him. And the church cannot be matured without following Jesus' example of maturing disciples.

◇

After looking at the Biblical examples of discipling, examining the specific discipling passages and logically connecting the premises, do you have any doubt that what we have termed "discipling relationships" are absolutely needed in order to fulfill Scripture and to bring about the evangelization of the world? It didn't take nearly this much evidence to convince me fifteen years ago, even though I knew the implications of accepting discipleship. I was compelled by Scripture and logic to embark on a journey that took me far, far away from familiar surroundings and lifetime comfort zones. The price I paid seemed high at the time, but the rewards have been beyond description, even beyond comprehension. The Scriptures are quite clear to all who would read them with a heart to obey.

Ultimately, we are discipled by God. Passages like Romans 8:28-29 and Hebrews 12:5-11 make it clear that God works through every aspect of our lives to help us become more like his Son. However, the discipling of one person by another is an integral part of God's plan for our lives and a key to fulfilling the mission of God on earth. I am my brother's keeper, and I am to let someone be my keeper. This has been God's will from the beginning. Let's pull out all the stops and dedicate ourselves to it as fully as did Jesus, Paul, Timothy and all others who have been determined to change their world. Lost souls are waiting for us to do it.

^{part}two

BEING A DISCIPLE OF JESUS

chapter four

BEING DISCIPLED
Jesus Is the Focus

Being discipled is a "Jesus thing," in that we are doing what he modeled and commanded for the purpose of becoming more like him and helping others to do the same. He is our example to imitate and the constant focus of all discipling efforts. Without this focus, discipling will become no more than a tradition at best and a burden at worst. In this chapter we will focus on Jesus and pose the question: "What does it mean to be a disciple?" His answer: to follow a leader, to follow on his terms, and to follow for training. As the voice from heaven in essence told other would-be disciples, "This is God's Son; listen to him."

To Follow a Leader

During the centuries leading up to Christ, the idea of following a leader for the purpose of becoming like him was quite in vogue. Aristotle had his disciples and Plato his. Their disciples committed themselves to following these famous leaders, intent on learning everything about them, imitating their behavior and espousing their philosophies. We independent Westerners have a difficult time with the concept. We pride ourselves on not becoming very much like those from whom we learn. We want to be our own man, to make our own unique mark in the world. At the very least, we are eclectic in our learning approach, taking a few ideas from one person and a few from the next.

The Jews in Jesus' day employed much the same method of training as did the famous philosophers. Leading rabbis had their little groups who followed them through the daily tasks, straining to pick up every tidbit of wisdom that might drop from their lips. Paul had been tutored in this fashion at the feet of probably the most famous rabbi of his time in Jerusalem. He spoke of this training in Acts 22:3:

> "I am a Jew, born in Tarsus of Cilicia, but brought up in this city. Under Gamaliel I was thoroughly trained in the law of our fathers and was just as zealous for God as any of you are today."

John the Baptist had a definite group of disciples who followed him and learned from him. Therefore, when Jesus came on the scene in his public ministry, it was not unusual that he would have had his own entourage of disciples following him to learn from him as their Master.

Certainly, he came forward like a rabbi, calling men to follow him. Unlike his Jewish counterparts, he broke through racial, ethical and national barriers in gaining adherents. Following him meant facing the same dangers he faced because you would be identified as his disciple and thus treated exactly as he was treated. Thomas understood this principle, once remarking to the other apostles "Let us also go, that we may die with him" (John 11:16). Similarly, Peter and the other apostles understood the implication of being his disciples, as seen in Matthew 26:35: "But Peter declared, 'Even if I have to die with you, I will never disown you.' And all the other disciples said the same."

The key concept to learn from these examples is that following someone as his disciple did not simply mean that you followed only to acquire some good philosophy. You were committing your life to being very closely identified with him to the point that whatever victories and defeats he had, you shared. In a real sense you gave up your identity and became an extension of him. In the Jewish system, given time and growth, you could advance to your master's status, but in Christ's system, you would always be his disciple.

With this background in mind, certain passages become crystal clear:

> I have been crucified with Christ and I no longer live, but Christ lives in me. (Galatians 2:20a)

> "A student is not above his teacher, but everyone who is fully trained will be like his teacher." (Luke 6:40)

> "Remember the words I spoke to you: 'No servant is greater than his master.' If they persecuted me, they will persecute you also. If they

> obeyed my teaching, they will obey yours
> also." (John 15:20)

And the beauty of following *this* Rabbi is that we end up not only becoming like him in this life, but being with him in the next:

> "Whoever serves me must follow me; and
> where I am, my servant also will be. My
> Father will honor the one who serves me."
> (John 12:26)

> "And if I go and prepare a place for you, I will
> come back and take you to be with me that
> you also may be where I am." (John 14:3)

Men discipling other men has only one aim: to help disciples of Jesus become more like him. He is the ultimate leader that we are to follow and emulate. We must keep in mind that although we are disciplers, there is only one Discipler, and all of our efforts must be to exalt him by discipling those in our care into his image.

To Follow on His Terms
Defining Relationships

Since Jesus is also the one Rabbi (meaning "Master" or "Teacher") we must follow him on *his* terms. In this vein, we must understand his terms by both definition and commitment. John's Gospel provides us with three specific definitions of what it means to follow Jesus. All three passages in which the definitions are found have to do with relationships (not a surprise!).

Relationship with Christ

The first has to do with our relationship with Christ:

> To the Jews who had believed him, Jesus said,
> "If you hold to my teaching, you are really my
> disciples. Then you will know the truth, and
> the truth will set you free." (John 8:31-32)

Jesus makes it clear that our relationship with him is dependent on our following his teachings. None can claim to be disciples who are not studying and obeying his word. In Luke 6:46, he stated "Why do you call me, 'Lord, Lord,' and do not do what I say?"

It is only when we are obedient to Jesus' teaching that the truth can be known. Contrary to the approach of Jewish rabbis, his approach was never intellectual, but always experiential. The truth of Jesus is pragmatic—it works. Since the basic definition of the word "disciple" is "one who follows in order to learn," we cannot really learn the deeper spiritual truths without first obeying as a means to learning. Do not expect everything taught by Jesus to make sense unless you are willing to obey it. He has orchestrated discipleship to demand that we must go beyond logic before his truths become apparent. Once we make the necessary "leap of faith," we are blessed with both understanding and the freedom which it brings. Therefore, let's make sure we comprehend the sequence of being a true disciple of Jesus: (1) initial belief in him, (2) holding to his teaching (studying and obeying it), (3) understanding it at the deeper spiritual level through experiencing it, and then (4) being freed from the bondage to sin that ignorance produces.

Relationship with Other Disciples

According to Jesus, a second aspect of discipleship has to do with our relationship with our brothers and sisters in the church:

> "A new command I give you: Love one another. As I have loved you, so you must love one another. By this all men will know that you are my disciples, if you love one another." (John 13:34-35)

The injunction to love was not new, in that the whole Old Testament was based on it (Matthew 22:36-40), but the type of love taught by Jesus was new. It was a love between brothers patterned after the depth of love he had demonstrated to them. Such love went far beyond anything the apostles had ever imagined. Once when Jesus had shown them the extent of forgiveness inherent in such love, they could only reply, "Increase our faith!" (Luke 17:1-5).

Further, this "new" love was a love designed to convince others that followers of Jesus were really his disciples. In order for this to happen, the love between believers has to be radically different than the love experienced in the world, even in the closest of families. How can it be this radically different? In a passage that is clearly messianic, Isaiah prophesied about these kinds of relationships:

> The wolf will live with the lamb,
>> the leopard will lie down with the goat,
> the calf and the lion and the yearling together;
>> and a little child will lead them.
> The cow will feed with the bear,
>> their young will lie down together,
>> and the lion will eat straw like the ox.
> The infant will play near the hole of the cobra,
>> and the young child put his hand into the
>>> viper's nest.
> They will neither harm nor destroy
>> on all my holy mountain,
> for the earth will be full of the knowledge of
>> the LORD
>> as the waters cover the sea. (Isaiah 11:6-9)

Isaiah 2:1-4 (when compared to Acts 1 and 2) helps us see that the "holy mountain" in Isaiah's vision is God's kingdom established by Jesus. As we see in the powerful metaphors of Isaiah 11 above, the relationships in this kingdom were going to be strikingly unique. In it would be found all kinds of people relating as brothers and sisters who could never have been united in the world.

The apostles were a great demonstration of the principle. There was Simon the Zealot, who hated everything about the Roman Empire, and Matthew, who worked for the Romans exacting taxes from his own people. In the world, these two would have been the worst of enemies, but in the church, they united for a greater cause. Within the group were two sets of brothers, who, in the world, would likely have been consumed with jealousy and envy, but who, in the kingdom, were brothers twice born, laboring side by side.

About a year ago, I listened as a brother named Curt shared at a church service about growing up as a black child in the South. As he described examples from his life about the racially prejudiced treatment he had received, even as a boy, I was shocked and saddened. He talked about how he had grown to hate whites, a hate which continued until he was middle-aged. Finally he was invited to visit a meeting of the body of Christ by a friend. While there, he saw a very racially mixed crowd, but he wasn't favorably impressed—he just wanted to leave and never come back. But some time after he had visited that Sunday, his wife Carol had a baby, and some people from the church (blacks and whites) kept bringing food to them and serving in other ways. Finally, the walls of hatred began to fall and Curt's heart began to soften. He started attending church regularly and began studying the Bible. After a while, both he and Carol were baptized into Christ as disciples.

I didn't know Curt well, but after he had finished sharing, I felt compelled to talk to him. I found him in the foyer and started trying to talk with him, but my emotions were welling up in me so strongly that all I could do for awhile was hug him and cry. My feelings were mixed, but very strong. I felt something of the hurt he must have felt to have been treated terribly simply because of his skin color. I felt grateful to my parents, who did not burden me with racial prejudice, although we were Southerners. Mostly, I felt wonderfully thankful to be in the kingdom of God, experiencing the love of disciples, who are determined to reject all of the world's prejudices by loving like Jesus commanded. Since that time, Curt and I have become very good friends and have shared some great times together.

Those of us who have returned to the Master's pattern for discipleship, see daily the love between the wolves and the lambs; the leopards and the goats; the calves and the lions; the cows and the bears; and the children and the cobras. This Jesus-love is a reality, not a theory, and may God be praised for it!

Relationship to the World

The third aspect of discipleship that we find in John's Gospel concerns our relationship to the world, whom we are trying to reach for Christ.

> "This is to my Father's glory, that you bear much fruit, showing yourselves to be my disciples." (John 15:8)

Fruit-bearing is the result of remaining in Christ, according to the earlier context of the passage. To remain in Christ means that we are ever growing to become like him, and certainly if we are like him, we will have his heart to "seek and to save what was lost" (Luke 19:10). Clearly, if we abide in Christ, we will bear fruit, and if we do not bear fruit, then we are no longer abiding in him. But what is the "fruit" under consideration?

Through the years, I have heard some very interesting discussions about whether the fruit here was the "fruit of the Spirit" mentioned in Galatians 5:22-23 or the fruit of evangelism. In one sense, the answer is simply yes. If we abide in Christ, we will certainly have both types.

Thus, to be a disciple of Jesus, according to the definitions in John's Gospel, we must be totally committed to relationships: a relationship with Jesus, based on holding to his teaching by learning and obeying it; a relationship with others in the kingdom which far surpasses love in the world, hurdling all barriers known to mankind; and a relationship with the world as we harvest them for Christ. Therefore, to be discipled means that we are going to be fully trained to be like Jesus in these fundamental areas.

Defining Commitment

Just as John was concerned with defining relationships in the disciple's life, Luke is concerned with defining the commitment. In Luke 9:22 Jesus warned his apostles that he was going to be killed and then rise from the dead. From other accounts, we know that the apostles had a difficult time accepting the truth of Jesus' warning. He then proceeded to elaborate about their fate if they continued to follow him, making it clear that these words were not reserved for the apostles, but for any person in any age who would follow him as a disciple:

> Then he said to them all: "If anyone would come after me, he must deny himself and take up his cross daily and follow me. For whoever wants to save his life will lose it, but whoever loses his life for me will save it." (Luke 9:23-24)

"Take up your cross daily." I think that many of us miss the point here. It certainly does not refer to the troubles in life which are common to man, Christian or non-Christian. I have heard people say, regarding their aches and pains, "This is my cross to bear." Admittedly, their physical challenges may be hard to bear, but this application is not what Jesus had in mind. On the other hand, the spiritual challenges of commitment to the church are not what he referred to either. Some church people seem to think that church attendance, spiritual group meetings, giving, and sharing their faith are to be equated with "cross bearing." Not true. Those activities are a privilege, and if they seem a burden to you, then you need to be open, ask for help and repent of a lack of gratitude.

Cross bearing meant to Jesus the biggest spiritual challenge he could possibly face. Yes, the cross meant persecution, and it meant death. But it was more than those things to him, because it carried the spiritual implications of his bearing the sins of the world. The challenge was so overwhelming that in anticipation of it, he agonized to the point of sweating blood (Luke 22:44). While it is true that the cross always includes "death to self," it places before us our most formidable challenge. And it must be remembered that not bearing it is not an option, no matter how daunting the challenge.

The rich young ruler (Luke 18:18-25) was called to face his highest hurdle, a love for money. Whenever any of us draws a line and says in effect to God, "This far and no further," God is going to introduce him to a cross with that very issue emblazoned at the top of it. Where have you drawn lines in your life? For many, it is a love for money and materialism. Being called to give liberally on a weekly basis or to sacrifice for special contributions exposes hearts, and many fail the test. For others, it is a certain job, or a relationship in their family or with a member of the opposite sex, or some hobby or entertainment, or any one of many other allurements of the world.

One of the most serious challenges to carrying the cross of Christ is to get out of our comfort zones. To say, "I can't do that," or "I would never do that," or "I would never go there or live there" is to guarantee that Jesus is going to come after you on that very point. Bearing a cross daily must mean that we will draw no lines anywhere in our lives. Although the threat of persecution is a scary one, fear cannot be allowed to determine our level of discipleship. It is total commitment or nothing (in God's eyes). He is either Lord of all or Lord not at all. The commitment of a disciple demands no less.

The well-known passage in Luke 14:25-33 is perhaps the most lucid regarding the commitment of being a disciple.[1] Here, Jesus begins by reiterating the demand to carry our cross, but moves quickly to saying that we must "hate" our families. Of course Jesus is not speaking literally here. The man who called us to love our enemies does not want to us to do the opposite to our families. He is using hyperbole to get our attention. Whatever may be said about his statements here, no disciple can allow family to determine what he does as a disciple. If we love family, even mother or father, more than we love Jesus, we are not worthy of him (Matthew 10:37).

I received a letter recently from a woman whose husband is not a disciple. He was giving her a difficult time about her commitment and was working hard to get her to make compromises. He wanted her to go with him to a traditional church which does not practice discipleship and leave the discipling ministry she was in. I tried explaining to her the difference in making concessions and compromises. Compromises are concerned with going against strong convictions in the more significant areas (like hers), while concessions concern the smaller issues of preference. Compromises encourage those with whom they are made to seek even more compromises. Concessions tend to build appreciation and bridges of further communication and understanding. I have seen many family members turn from being persecutors of disciples and become disciples themselves, but I have never

[1] For a more detailed treatment of this passage, see chapter 6 in my book, *The Victory of Surrender—Second Edition* (Woburn, Mass.: DPI, 1999), 64-72.

seen this happen when compromise was made by the disciple—never, not even once!

Showing compromise and sentimentality toward family is the worst thing possible for them. Just think about how Jesus dealt with his family before they became his disciples. As recorded in Mark 3:20-21, we find that his family came to "take charge of him, for they said, 'He is out of his mind.'" Do you understand the situation here? Jesus' mother, Mary, and his brothers thought that he was *insane!* I know that he loved them intensely and wanted them to see the truth that he was preaching. So how did he show his love and his desire for their salvation? We find out a few verses later:

> Then Jesus' mother and brothers arrived. Standing outside, they sent someone in to call him. A crowd was sitting around him, and they told him, "Your mother and brothers are outside looking for you."
>
> "Who are my mother and my brothers?" he asked.
>
> Then he looked at those seated in a circle around him and said, "Here are my mother and my brothers! Whoever does God's will is my brother and sister and mother." (Mark 3:31-35)

Just picture this occasion—the family arrives to get Jesus, but are too embarrassed by what they think of him to even go inside after him. They think he has gone crazy and is inside indoctrinating a little cult group. Upon being told that his family is outside, Jesus makes his point about who his real family is (and it was not they!). He would not even go outside and try to placate them in the least. As far as the text is concerned, he just kept teaching those who had a heart to learn and left his family outside until they decided to leave or until he was quite through with what he came to do.

Can you imagine what must have been going through the minds of Mary, James, Joseph, Judas and Simon? (His brother's names can be found in Mark 6:3.) If they thought Jesus was crazy before they arrived, just what were they thinking after this little confrontation? The point is clear—disciples are those who make Jesus their master and will not compromise their convictions for anyone, even the closest of family.

In our Luke 14 passage, Jesus says three times that unless we meet certain conditions, we "cannot be his disciple." The first two instances are in verse 26 concerning cross bearing and in verse 27 concerning "hating" family. The third instance is in verse 33, which says, "In the same way, any of you who does not give up everything he has cannot be my disciple." The NASV translates it "give up all his own possessions." Whatever we have ultimately belongs to God, even the money he gives us to manage. How we view money and possessions is one of the best possible indicators of our discipleship.

Once, I received advice about dealing with my possessions that cost me a great deal. The advice was not good, as it turned out, and some things were not handled well in the whole situation. But I opted to drop it fairly quickly, in the tenor of 1 Corinthians 6:7, "Why not rather be wronged?" To be candid, the situation really challenged my heart—for a while. But Luke 14:33 stayed before my eyes, and I could not rationalize around it. I had to reach the point where two basic truths settled my mind once for all. One, I knew I had some greed in my heart, and although I could have defended my actions in a reasonable manner, I knew deep down that greed was not absent. Two, I knew that God was in control and that if I needed the money, he could figure out any number of ways to get it back to me. Looking back to that time, I am "richer" for the experience. I grew in my trust in God and in forgiveness for men, and lost a large amount of greed in the process.

Obviously, we are responsible for the decisions we make. We must always think through the advice we are given, and talk through input that we do not understand. We must live with our decisions to accept or reject the advice of others. But the issue is this: Do we trust God to work through people? Where is your trust? Where is your humility? Are you willing to get your heart tested by God through men? Are you a disciple or not? The answer is determined by how you are living out the definitions found in John and the commitment found in Luke.

To Follow for Training

"Take my yoke upon you and learn from me, for I am gentle and humble in heart, and you will find rest for your souls" (Matthew 11:29). Following Jesus has as its goal our training to become more and more like him. The apostles understood this principle, which made them eager (at times) to learn. As they watched his life unfold before them on a daily basis, they were anxious to grasp all of the lessons he modeled. They observed his remarkable prayer life, and they said "Lord, teach us to pray, just as John taught his disciples" (Luke 11:1). "Lord, teach us!" This is the cry of a true disciple. We do not follow him merely to end up in heaven with him; we follow him in order to learn everything we can about carrying out his mission on earth. And for the accomplishment of his mission, we must be trained via the discipling process.

Most of this chapter has dealt with the vertical aspect of discipleship (our commitment to Christ). We have taken that path for two basic reasons, one Biblical and one practical. The Biblical issue is that the terminology relating to discipleship is primarily directed at the vertical relationship. The practical issue is founded on this Biblical emphasis: without first having a sound vertical relationship, the horizontal relationships, in which discipling occurs, cannot function effectively. In a word, we must really want to be discipled. A child who has been coerced into taking piano lessons will be a poor student regardless of the quality of the music teacher. On the other hand, a willing child will learn quickly, even from an inexperienced teacher. It is a question of motivation, isn't it? Similarly, if a person wants to be as much like Jesus as possible, discipling-partner relationships will be very welcome.

The discipling process is vital in training people in everything from how to pray, to how to study, to how to live a disciplined life, to how to deal Biblically with issues never mentioned specifically in the Bible (and there are several!). However, we will never be thus trained unless we desire to be trained.

About a year ago, I was unexpectedly treated to a golf lesson by a Christian golf professional who taught in one of the country's premier golf schools. He pointed out many things that I was doing wrong and even videotaped my swing to prove his point. I was fired-up for such an opportunity! He discipled me as a golfer for three hours, and I was overjoyed. Why? Because I love golf. Did I mind being critiqued? No, I loved it because my purpose was to improve. Just imagine what would happen if all disciples were as excited as that to improve as disciples in order to accomplish their purpose for Christ! They would welcome critique and absolutely love discipling—being trained to be their best for God! How do you feel about being discipled? Are you more fired-up about improving something like a golf swing than you are about improving as a representative of Jesus Christ?

Unless and until we have made a disciple's commitment to God, like the one described in this chapter, discipling by the people God puts into our lives will be a burden and not a blessing. Without total commitment to Christ as disciples, we will not seek the training we need, we will not grow, and the world will not be won. It is an all-or-nothing proposition.

God trains us, if we will let him, through circumstances, the Bible and the people he puts into our lives. But we must want it and want it badly. What does it mean to be a disciple? It means that we are totally committed to following a leader: Jesus, the master discipler. It means that we know his terms and are willing to follow them no matter what the consequences may be. We will obey and trust him to work out all the details of our lives. We will sign the spiritual blank check and then let him fill in all of the blanks.

And finally, being a disciple means that we will love being trained. If we are disciples, we will love being discipled. We will seek it out, submit joyfully to it, and trust God to refine our characters and to supply through others the specifics needed to fully utilize the general principles he has given in his word. Nothing is more practical and helpful than being trained as a disciple. Our joy level is tied inseparably to our growth level. Discipling keeps us growing, and therefore, it keeps us excited. We do not have to be saddled with ourselves for the rest of our lives, praise God! We can change more and more into his image, and as we do, we will be both happy and productive. Why be a dull, uninteresting, apathetic pool of mediocrity when you can be discipled to be like Jesus?

chapter **five**

BEING DISCIPLED
Why Is It Important?

Being discipled is important for a number of good
Biblical and practical reasons. It keeps us focused on life's
most essential goal: the pursuit of Jesus. It protects us
from Satan in that we become more aware of our own sinful tendencies through the helpful input of others. Finally,
it builds our character, as spirituality becomes the basis of
who we are and not simply what we do. If we are focused
on Jesus, protected from the onslaughts of Satan, developing a more spiritual character, then success is the
inevitable result. Let's examine each of these vital elements
involved in being discipled.

Discipling Keeps Us Focused

Staying focused as a disciple is no easy task. In the
Parable of the Soils, we find that if we stay faithful to
God past the "new Christian" stage, our biggest challenge
will then be to avoid getting choked by the cares of this
life. These challenges are constant. I have never known
any disciple who did not at times lose his focus and have
to be called back to "sold out" status once again. Being
discipled keeps us from wandering far, and it keeps us

from staying out of focus for long periods. But when there are so many things that we need to do, what is the key focus needed in our lives as disciples? The answer for me is two-fold. First, we need to become more and more like Jesus (1 Peter 2:21, 1 John 2:6). Second, we need to stay focused on his mission for us of seeking and saving the lost (Luke 19:10, Acts 20:24). Just about everything else grows out of these key areas. If I am concentrating on these, life goes well indeed. When I minimize either, my heart begins to harden and my spiritual life weakens.

Focused on the Imitation of Jesus

"Whoever claims to live in him must walk as Jesus did" (1 John 2:6). If I could point out one of our most glaring weaknesses in discipling, it would be in imitating Jesus. We have four Gospel accounts in the Bible for a reason: God wanted us to see in Jesus' life the demonstration of other Biblical teachings. Again, it is seeing teachings lived out in flesh and blood that helps us to learn the most effectively. I have a very strong conviction that all of us need to study the life of Jesus much more than we do. I also have a strong concern that much of our studying of his life is reserved mostly for individual "quiet time" study rather than with one another in our discipling relationships. We simply must spend the time thinking about how to apply Jesus' example to real-life situations in a way which makes the Biblical accounts come alive. These types of questions must become much more a part of our discipling times: "What would Jesus do in your situation?" "Why do you think so?" "Which example from Jesus' life most relates to your current problem?" There may be times when we are able to avoid the full impact of challenging Biblical commands because of a hardness of heart, but if we have any softness left, the example of Jesus will melt us.

John, the beloved apostle who walked closely with Jesus, left us with this charge:

> But if anyone obeys his word, God's love is truly made complete in him. This is how we know we are in him: Whoever claims to live in him must walk as Jesus did. (1 John 2:5-6)

Here are just some examples of subjects from Jesus life that we need to focus on.

- Assurances of Jesus ("Do not be afraid")
- Humility of Jesus
- Prayers of Jesus
- How Jesus Handled Interruptions
- Those Whom Jesus Touched
- Jesus' Intolerance of Hypocrisy
- What If Jesus Had Never Come?
- Titles and Names of Jesus in Scripture
- What Made Jesus Frustrated?
- How Did Jesus Deal with Disappointments?

- Jesus As the Door
        —As the Vine
        —As the Light
        —As the Teacher
        —As the Lamb of God
        —(many similar others)
- The Magnetism of Jesus
- Unexpected Reactions of Jesus
- Different Reactions to Jesus
- How He Related to Children, Older People, Women, the Pharisees, the Pagans, the Poor, the Physically Challenged, etc.
- Things That Amazed Jesus
- Jesus As High Priest
- What Made Jesus Joyful?
- What Made Jesus Angry?
- Jesus As Possessor of the Best Masculine Qualities
- Jesus As Possessor of the Best Feminine Qualities
- Jesus As a Disciple of the Father
- The Humanity of Jesus
- The Divinity of Jesus
- Those Whom Jesus Served

The most compelling reason to do anything is because Jesus would have done it. His heart is extensively revealed in the Gospels in ways that can change and direct our lives, but all of us are going to have to dig in much deeper than we are accustomed to digging. This digging should take place in our individual study and in our teaching, preaching and discipling of others. The more we use Scripture as we advise other people, the more impact for good it will have; and the more Jesus' example is our scriptural focus, the greater the heart changes thus produced.

Focused on the Mission of Jesus

Many directives are given to disciples, but none is more important than the command to go make more disciples and bring them to God. Jesus came into the world, carried out his ministry and ultimately died on the cross to seek and to save the lost. He woke up every morning thinking about this mission and shut his eyes at night with prayers for this mission controlling his heart. The Great Commission (or the Great Imperative) was the last thing which came from his lips before he ascended to heaven. We must daily imitate this heart and life. We are in a quest for souls, a battle with Satanic forces for the eternal destiny of countless millions.

As a minister prior to my discipling days, I at least paid homage to the concept that the Great Commission was indeed one of the most fundamental responsibilities we have on planet Earth. But I did not get the big picture until I saw in action those who practiced discipling.

After I became a part of a church where discipleship and discipling were the norm, I needed much help learning to become a better fisher of men. Most of that help came from people who were much younger than I (physically), but I loved learning from them. I have become much more effective through the years, and I am still trying to learn all

I can about affecting people like Jesus did. Much of what I need now is accountability—the kind we find in good discipling. People in most religious circles are not accustomed to any kind of spiritual accountability and might even be offended by the word. However, properly understood, the concept is Biblical and its practice very beneficial.

Jesus sent out the Twelve and the seventy-two on their missions and then had them report back to him for a "debriefing" of sorts. He wanted to make sure their attitudes were in the right place and that they had learned the lessons he intended for them to learn. Reporting in was a part of their training.

There is really nothing here that is surprising. Can you imagine any business in the world without some form of accountability? Can you imagine any school without it, or any family? In areas outside of religion, accountability is absolutely expected.

What determines the need for and the level of accountability in such life situations? The importance of the assigned task, pure and simple. What does the lack of accountability in most religious circles say about those groups? They do not view what they do as fundamentally important. However, disciples must view their work as radically important. Remember, we are imitating Jesus.

For disciples, accountability is designed simply to help us follow through with what we are already committed to doing. It should never be seen as a tool to make us do what we do not want to do. If we don't want to do what disciples are Biblically mandated to do, then we have a heart problem, and accountability is not going to help us until we have a change of heart. But I need accountability in evangelism. I wish that I had the same drive and focus Jesus had, but I do not always have it. I need brothers with whom I can talk and plan as we "spur one another on to love and good deeds." Knowing that others are going to ask me about my evangelism is very good—it spurs me on to do what my spirit wants to do, even when my flesh is weak.

Discipling helps keep us on track in following Jesus, as we are his co-workers to save the lost. Is discipling important? Absolutely, for without it, we strongly tend to lose our focus and Jesus' prime directive falls by the wayside. Be a disciple, be discipled, and stay focused!

Discipling Protects Us from Satan

"But encourage one another daily, as long as it is called Today, so that none of you may be hardened by sin's deceitfulness" (Hebrews 3:13). One clear purpose of discipling is to assist each other in resisting Satan. When I first was visiting churches that practiced discipling, I met a man in a controversial congregation who was writing a book defending the practice. He gave me a copy of the manuscript, which I took back home with me. A few days later, I started reading it and was shaken to my roots. I honestly don't remember too many details in the material, but I do remember what he said about discipling's potential to stop sin at the temptation level. For three days I read the manuscript, and literally could not sleep at night! My mind would not quit racing and my heart would not stop pounding. I could not stop thinking about how many people's lives would have been changed and how much pain and devastation could have been avoided had Biblical discipling been practiced.

I vowed to God that I would begin obeying his teaching about discipleship and learn as much about it as possible. I knew that in order to do these two things, I would have to accept the controversial nature of the subject and follow God rather than men. I made the decision to follow the Bible and its clear teaching about discipleship and discipling and let the chips fall where they would. Praise God, for my life has never been the same since. Only God knows how much sin and pain have been averted in my family by our dealing with sin at the temptation level.

Those who are not being open about their temptations are playing with spiritual dynamite. Every time I am open with another person about my sins and my temptations to sin, my heart breathes a sigh of relief. Delivered again, praise Jesus! Satan then has to retreat into his vile darkness and look for other souls to deceive.

Discipling Builds Our Character

Those who follow Jesus are called to make major changes in their lives. Paul put it this way in Ephesians 4:22-24:

> You were taught, with regard to your former way of life, to put off your old self, which is being corrupted by its deceitful desires; to be made new in the attitude of your minds; and to

> put on the new self, created to be like God in
> true righteousness and holiness.

Such a statement sounds great and what is described here is great, but anyone who has worked with people knows that such changes are not easily made. Paul is talking here about major character change, not just redecorating the exterior. Certainly, the Bible teaches that the Holy Spirit is involved in helping us make these changes (2 Corinthians 3:18), but it is clear from the sheer volume of "one another" texts (discussed in chapter 2) that we are to play a key role in each other's lives. A close look reveals that the Holy Spirit works through our relationships to help us make character changes we could not and would not make on our own (see, for example, 1 Corinthians 12).

We become who we are in two basic ways. First, we are born with certain qualities or certain tendencies in many areas of both capability and character. (While inheritance is not the total issue or the final word in who we become, it unquestionably is a factor.) Second, we are molded by our environment, particularly our closest relationships in that environment, like our family situations. Many possible combinations of inheritance and environment work together to make us who we are at any given point.

Our basic tendencies, which are inborn, can be good or bad. Our outside influences can be good or bad. In between the two extremes, neutral tendencies and influences are possible, but the extremes are the most important in understanding why we are as we are.

If I am born with a "bent" toward a given quality or ability, my "discipling" (atmosphere, influences) can alter it in a major way. If I have an inborn tendency for being an unselfish servant (and there are people like this), the "discipling" I receive will affect me significantly. If I have parents who are themselves unselfish and who actively direct me toward serving, I will likely end up as an unselfish person. On the other hand, if my parents are selfish and train me in selfishness (consciously or unconsciously), they can stifle the positive natural bent in my character.

On the other hand, suppose that I am born with very few tendencies toward unselfishness. A selfish environment will do nothing but make me more selfish. Clearly, two negatives do not a make a positive! However, a positive atmosphere of discipling (parents' example plus their training of the child) can significantly alter the natural tendency toward selfishness. Even with a natural inclination toward selfishness, I can become more unselfish and giving.

We were all born with a variety of strengths and weaknesses, and we have all been exposed to environments that have influenced those in various ways. But the Bible says in so many words, that even the best of us is a mess (Romans 3:23). When we become disciples, we make a conscious decision to put ourselves in an environment where the sinful tendencies will be discouraged and the godly tendencies will be encouraged and we should welcome any relationship that contributes to this environment. Satan is strong, sin is real, and we cannot develop righteousness without a serious commitment to it. Success in making changes will never be permanent by accident—it takes planning and perseverance.

The conclusion of the matter is that all of us need to develop an accurate view of our weaknesses, develop long-range and short-range plans for change, and put the plans into effect *daily*. Disciplers are invaluable in helping us see our weaknesses accurately, formulating practical plans on a weekly basis, and following through on a daily basis. If we have deep convictions about our weaknesses, a deep desire to change, a plan which includes discipling to help us change behavior, and a strong prayer life to allow God to change our hearts, we will change both character and actions. We will become more and more like Jesus.

One of the most practical definitions of discipling I ever heard came from my friend Douglas Arthur. He said "Discipling is gentle pressure—relentlessly applied!" Discipling involves pressure, but it is the welcome, gentle pressure of one who loves us and genuinely wants us to be our best for God. To achieve that lofty goal, the loving pressure must be applied consistently and without exception. Just think of how this approach relates to training children. If parents follow it, blessed indeed will be their children. And if discipleship partners follow it with each other, blessed will be our lives as we become more and more like our Pattern.

chapter six

BEING DISCIPLED
The Keys to Success

Being discipled refers to the close involvement of another person of the same sex in our lives for the purpose of helping us to become more like Jesus. It encompasses every aspect of life, that we might be well-rounded and mature. The more mature we become, the stronger influence we will exert in the lives of our brothers and sisters in Christ and in the lives of those who are not yet a part of his kingdom. But what are the keys? Which key qualities do we especially need if we are to gain everything possible from discipling and become mature as disciples?

Openness

Learning to open up at the emotional level was one of the most difficult hurdles I have ever crossed. Men in our culture have what appears to be a natural aversion to this level of communication. However, women are much more comfortable with it, and most wives deeply desire to experience this kind of communication with their husbands.

When we read through the Bible looking for openness at the feeling level, we will be impressed. God sets the pace, as might be expected! He lays his heart out time after time. Jesus did the same, as did many other Biblical characters. Especially revealing is a study of Paul's life. Try reading the book of 2 Corinthians with the purpose of studying Paul's levels of communication. His openness about his struggles and the terms of endearment he used toward others definitely call us men much higher in being expressive and vulnerable.[1]

Some years ago, I learned that the more vulnerable you are, the faster you grow. A minister friend heard me speak on this subject in a traditional church when I was first learning to be open, and he made a statement to his congregation that I've never forgotten: "We come to church hiding behind our little shells of protection, and about all we do together is bump shells and go home." We desperately need to get out of our shells and enjoy the growth that is ours for the taking!

What does all of this have to do with discipling? Everything! Discipling relationships are designed by God to meet our need to be open with our feelings. We humans are such people-pleasers and conflict-avoiders that we have "stuffed" tons of attitudes inside, to our detriment. Our need to be open at the feeling level can hardly be overstated. Such vulnerability blesses us in two ways. First, it can strengthen our self image and confidence. Second, it limits the effects of sin, which when locked up inside, destroys our souls.

As stated earlier, learning to be open was very difficult for me and at times is still difficult. But I am committed

---

[1] For additional information on this topic, see Marty Wooten *Power in Weakness* (Woburn, Mass.: DPI, 1997).

to being open because the results are highly beneficial. I can remember a number of specific times when my attitudes were terrible and my mood horrible and the thought of opening up was painful. Yet, after fighting through and doing it, I felt on top of the world in a very short time. Prior to getting it all out, Satan caused my imagination to go wild. *If I let others know what I am really like, then they won't like me (or respect me, or love me). In fact, I'll probably be asked to leave the ministry!* Of course, none of these things happened. Actually, it was quite the opposite, as people responded to my openness (and confession of sin) with love and grace. No wonder Satan hates our openness! Clearing out our hearts has an unbelievable effect on our moods and attitudes.

But keep in mind the main purpose of openness. It is designed to bring our hearts out in the open, so that our discipleship partners can help to spiritually tune us up. Sometimes after opening up with bad attitudes and getting corrected, some think or say, "Well, at least I was open. I don't see why you are on my case now!" Openness about attitudes doesn't make them correct. Being honest is absolutely essential, true enough, but essential because our hearts can be seen clearly and then helped.

If you are not now totally committed to being open with your life—victories and defeats, dreams and fears, temptations and sins—then please repent and make that commitment now. You will never be a happy and successful disciple without it.

Seeking Advice

Seeking advice is one of the greatest needs and blessings in a disciple's life. Outside the kingdom, just where would you go to receive good advice about life? The last time I looked, I did not notice many truly successful people out there (at least not successful in the areas that are most important to me!). But praise God that in the kingdom, great advice abounds. Many scriptures point out the tremendous value of seeking godly advice. Here are but a few, all from the book of Proverbs:

- The way of a fool seems right to him,
    but a wise man listens to advice. (12:15)
- Pride only breeds quarrels,
    but wisdom is found in those who
        take advice. (13:10)
- Plans fail for lack of counsel,
    but with many advisers they succeed.
    (15:22)
- Listen to advice and accept instruction,
    and in the end you will be wise. (19:20)
- Make plans by seeking advice;
    if you wage war, obtain guidance. (20:18)
- Perfume and incense bring joy to the heart,
    and the pleasantness of one's friend
        springs from his earnest counsel. (27:9)

The last one in the list is especially appropriate in describing the relationship between discipling partners.

Our counsel for one another grows out of a loving friendship and an earnest desire to help each other grow and experience joy. I don't know about you, but I have already made enough mistakes in my life. Seeking advice has spared me much heartache. Often our decisions may not have earth-shaking consequences, but in being followers of Jesus (who did everything well: Mark 7:37), we should want to make the very best choices. In fact, once we gain a reasonable amount of spiritual perspective, most of our choices will not be between good and bad, but between good, better and best. Paul described this truth in these words:

> And this is my prayer: that your love may abound more and more in knowledge and depth of insight, so that you may be able to discern what is best and may be pure and blameless until the day of Christ. (Philippians 1:9-10)

Several practical suggestions are in order here to help you obtain and use advice in the best way.

1. Pray that God will really work through those from whom you are going to seek advice, that he will give you and them wisdom.
2. Seek advice in all areas of life, especially if you are a newer disciple. Get advice about priorities, time usage, spending time with old friends, evangelism, entertainment options, finances and the like. In doing this, you will learn the areas in which your judgment is best and worst. In the areas where

your judgment is weakest, you will know to make sure to seek plenty of advice in the future. It is difficult to conceive of getting too much advice, so tend to seek much, not little.

3. The weightier the consequences of your decisions, the more advice you should seek. However, when seeking counsel from a number of people, be careful not to just keep asking additional people until you hear what you want to hear! It is normal to enter the decision-making mode with some preconceived ideas, but our hearts must be open in order to really consider what others say. If I receive conflicting advice, I go back to the parties who differ and attempt to find a way for us all to end up on the same page. Certainly, you should give much heavier weight to the mature disciples in your life who know you the best.

4. Keep your heart open to the advice of others, but don't glibly accept it if your heart isn't there. On one occasion, I remember seeking some very important advice from a very mature leader. Although I did not feel settled about going the route he suggested in the guise of being a "good disciple," I followed the advice. The results were not good. Later I mentioned the outcome to him and confessed that I had not felt comfortable with his advice and told him why. He responded by saying that if I had given him the benefit of hearing those reasons earlier, his advice would have

been different. Good point. From this I learned to keep talking until I feel settled and both of us end up in agreement, if at all possible (and just about always, it is). And I have also learned that to keep praying for wisdom throughout the whole process helps me to get settled out emotionally and in touch with what may be keeping me from being comfortable with the advice.

A Submissive Spirit

To possess a submissive spirit is to possess a very spiritual quality, but since it is spiritual, it is also unnatural. We tend to grow up trusting no one nearly as much as we trust ourselves. We think we are the center of the universe, and we like being in control. If we have been hurt significantly by authority figures in our lives, submission is all the harder. In any event, one of our most pervasive sins is pride, and pride is poisonous to submission. The antidote is obviously a good dose of humility.

Do you want to be a wise person in the sight of God? Then develop a submissive spirit, as James tells us:

> But the wisdom that comes from heaven is first of all pure; then peace-loving, considerate, submissive, full of mercy and good fruit, impartial and sincere. (James 3:17)

This development is based on accepting at the emotional level what is taught in 1 Peter 2:18-3:8. As the account begins, slaves are given a startling command: "Slaves, submit yourselves to your masters with all respect, not only to those who are good and considerate, but also to those who are harsh" (1 Peter 2:18). Our human nature cries out against God's teaching here, as we say, "Wait a minute—submitting to a good master who deserves respect may be all right, but this business of respecting a harsh one doesn't make any sense at all!"

However, the disciple doesn't practice submission simply because it makes worldly sense. We do it not because of who the master is, but because of who the Master is! We do it because of *whose* we are and who *we* are. How are we able to do such a challenging thing? As we continue reading the passage, we find the answer: Imitate Christ. He did not retaliate when mistreated because he had entrusted himself to God, really believing that God was in control and would work out everything for his good. (Romans 8:28 does say that, doesn't it?) The same principle was next applied to women and their need to submit to their husband's leadership (1 Peter 3:1-6); then to husbands who needed to submit to their wife's needs (1 Peter 3:7); and finally to each other in the church (1 Peter 3:8). The latter verse puts it this way:

> Finally, all of you, live in harmony with one another; be sympathetic, love as brothers, be compassionate and humble.

You see, the submissive spirit is the umbrella under which we will be protected and led by God.

Biblically, we are obligated to practice submission in all kinds of relationships in the world (bosses, law officers and other public officials, teachers, etc.). If this submission to worldly authority is to be carried out with "all respect," then how much more should we have submissive spirits toward those in the church, especially those who are trying to help us grow. Remember that being discipled keeps us in a humble mode, and God will always bless humility.

When I first heard of discipling partners, I thought it sounded pretty good—as an older leader, I could disciple younger leaders in the kingdom. When I put two and two together and realized that I would also need to be discipled, then my pride rose up a bit! However, once I started receiving the blessings of having a submissive spirit in this relationship and in relationships in the kingdom generally, I felt tremendously better.

A most important passage for understanding this need for submission is 1 Peter 5:5-6:

> Young men, in the same way be submissive to those who are older. All of you, clothe yourselves with humility toward one another, because,
>
> "God opposes the proud
>   but gives grace to the humble."
>
> Humble yourselves, therefore, under God's mighty hand, that he may lift you up in due time.

Several lessons stand out in these verses. First, younger men need to have submissive spirits toward older men, and it makes sense that this principle applies to both chronological and spiritual age. Second, we all should be clothed with humility toward one another, regardless of age and maturity distinctions. Third, humbling ourselves under God's mighty hand is done by practicing humility with one another. (The "therefore" makes this point clear.) Fourth, we will be lifted up at the proper time by God. He always blesses humility, and humility is demonstrated almost exclusively by how we relate to other human beings. Be submissive to those in your life, trusting that God will work through them (and if need be, in spite of them!). And get ready to receive blessings like never before!

Imitation

One evidence of being humble is the desire to imitate Christ in others. Imitation is without question the fastest way to learn how to do something, be it a golf swing or a culinary procedure. A number of years ago, I taught in a minister's training school. In a preaching class, I assigned topics for speeches of different types and lengths. Once, in delivering a full-length sermon, a student preached a sermon that he and most of the students had heard me preach about the second coming of Christ. That student imitated my preaching very closely in both content and delivery. In the critique session afterwards, one of his fellow students was very critical of his imitating of me.

Personally, I thought he was a very wise student because Jesus himself said, "A student is not above his teacher, but everyone who is fully trained will be like his teacher" (Luke 6:40). Maybe you would think it coincidental, but the imitator in this story has gone on to become a very successful evangelist in the kingdom of God, and the critic has been through divorce and many other rough times. The issue is pride and humility, wouldn't you think?

If we trust that God has put us with discipleship partners in order to help us grow, then we will want to learn from them by imitating. The Bible amply emphasizes the need to learn from one another via the imitation process. Imitating another disciple takes humility, and since pride can cause us to shy away from imitation, I am including a number of passages to help us get the picture.

- "Come, follow me," Jesus said, "and I will make you fishers of men." (Jesus, Mark 1:17)

- "I tell you the truth, anyone who has faith in me will do what I have been doing." (Jesus, John 14:12b)

- "My sheep listen to my voice; I know them, and they follow me." (Jesus, John 10:27)

- Therefore I urge you to imitate me. (Paul, 1 Corinthians 4:16)

- Follow my example, as I follow the example of Christ. (Paul, 1 Corinthians 11:1)

- Join with others in following my example, brothers, and take note of those who live according to the pattern we gave you. (Paul, Philippians 3:17)

- You became imitators of us and of the Lord; in spite of severe suffering, you welcomed the message with the joy given by the Holy Spirit. (Paul, 1 Thessalonians 1:6)

- For you yourselves know how you ought to follow our example. We were not idle when we were with you. (Paul, 2 Thessalonians 3:7)

- Remember your leaders, who spoke the word of God to you. Consider the outcome of their way of life and imitate their faith. (Hebrews 13:7)

Certainly we are not to imitate in another's life that which is not Christlike, but we are to learn as much as possible from them. A good deal of what we learn will be along very practical lines. Perhaps we need a better sense of humor or a better sense of soberness. Maybe they have more Bible knowledge than we, or if less, more practical wisdom about how to apply it. Mark it down: You are teamed up with your discipleship partner for God's reasons, and you need to trust that fact and learn everything possible. Without humility, you are going to miss out on learning some very valuable lessons.

In this chapter I have given you some of the keys to being successfully discipled. Focus on these. Go after your weaknesses. Bring your attitudes into line with the things I have described here, and you will be blessed. Do not look at the problems your discipler has. Do not blame him or her for your condition. Listen to what God is calling you to, and take hold of these keys with all your heart. You will be amazed at how God will work in your discipling relationship to transform your life.

chapter seven

BEING DISCIPLED
The Practicals That Help It Work

Being discipled is all about attitude. Those who have a great attitude are grateful for discipling; they grow from discipling; they see their lives and their relationships blessed. The four keys we looked at in the previous chapter could be called attitude keys. Wander from them and it will not be long before you are spiritually weakened. Stay with them and you will experience the power of God. But now that we have looked at the crucial attitudes, it is time to examine some practicals that will enable God to further bless your discipling relationships.

Appreciate Organization

Everyone's business ends up being no one's business. Occasionally some of us react negatively to the organizing and scheduling of spiritual activities, reasoning that relationships should just happen naturally. In our hectic society, nothing good seems to just "happen." For the most part, I find that times with my wife for dating or talking through issues must be planned. Oh, sure, sometimes we have a good talk on the spur of the moment, but if we left it up to happenstance, it would not occur nearly often enough. My phone calls to our children and other close relatives don't seem to just "happen." Let's face it—we live in a world of overflowing schedules, and we are going to have to organize if we are to make the best use of our time.

In order to encourage discipleship, churches have to organize so that everyone has a discipling partner. We need to be grateful that someone cares enough to make this happen. Several factors are considered by the leaders who are organizing discipling relationships: geography (allowing the discipleship partners to get time together more easily); ministry group; age and maturity (chronological and spiritual); marital status (marrieds need to be paired up with marrieds when possible); leadership roles and potential; special needs (transportation, physical challenges, family challenges, etc.); and perhaps others. Consideration is given in pairing people up who can really help one another grow. Of course, those inclined to be negative about such arrangements would say, "You can't legislate friendships!" True enough, but disciples can be organized in a way that affords powerful, spiritual friendships the opportunity to develop. A part of the problem reflected in the previous negative comment is worldly thinking: "Who am I *naturally* drawn to?" But in the kingdom, we are all brothers and sisters and need to learn to be a close family. The relationships which at first seem unnatural are likely the ones in which we grow most!

Biblically, the necessity for organization can be seen by studying passages like Exodus 18 and Acts 6. Organization is always needed to make any group function effectively. So appreciate organization in the church; God is behind it.

Think Friendship

Discipleship partners should be or should become great friends. Some come into the kingdom with mistaken attitudes about close relationships. They think that they can only have one best friend at a time and that being close to one person rules out other close relationships. Our model for loving is God, who loves everyone incredibly more than they can imagine! Therefore, as we imitate him, we will learn to love more and more people more and more deeply. But we must begin with the few, and in this case, the one.

Worldly friendships are formed almost solely on the basis of sharing things in common. In other words, if you can really identify with a person, then (and only then) do you have a foundation for developing a really close relationship. However, when we come into the kingdom, we find ourselves in a "melting pot" of diverse people and personality types. We then begin to learn how to relate to all different kinds, many of whom would never have been our close friends outside of Christ—which is the beauty of being in the kingdom! Our relational abilities will be nurtured and refined in some amazing ways.

How do we develop best-friend spiritual relationships? We start with the determination to do it, regardless of the challenges involved. Then, we begin developing the friendship by sharing our lives in at least these four ways:

(1) opening up our hearts to one another, (2) serving together, (3) praying together and (4) playing together.

Direct, open communication, including confession of temptations and sins, is key. Openness makes it all come together—heart to heart and soul to soul. Working side by side in the kingdom in studying with non-Christians or counseling or serving others will draw you close. Praying together is a good beginning step in learning what is in each other's heart. We have a hard time faking where or who we are when we are talking to God. Playing together is an essential part of the bonding process. Loosen up and have fun doing something both of you enjoy. I love getting out on the golf course with a discipleship partner or playing Hearts (the card game). Being competitive, I often have to repent of something before the round or game is over, but that's a part of spiritual male bonding!

In general, forget the idea that friendship must come naturally or else it is not real. Friendships that we work to build can become some of the most special ones in our lives. When, for organizational and ministry reasons, you have to change discipling relationships, don't lose the friendship you have built. You will not get as much time with a person who moves on to become someone else's discipling partner, but keep them in your heart. Call them, write them and stay in touch.

Keep Expectations Reasonable

One of the most consistent challenges in relationships revolves around expectations. It doesn't matter whether we are talking about relationships between marriage partners or between parent and child or between any other two people, expectations are a *huge* issue. Often we do not even know what our expectations are until someone doesn't meet them. In discipleship partner relationships, certain unrealistic expectations can creep in and induce needless pain.

The first of those is the expectation that my discipling partner be a miracle worker in helping my character to change! Habits are not so difficult that they cannot be broken; avoiding something for about thirty days may loosen the grip of even a seriously bad habit. But character changes are on a different scale. Our characters have been formed over many years and resist being reformed. Discipleship partners are indispensable in making these changes, but they are only helpers and surely not the total cure.

The Hebrew writer gave us a most helpful insight as he described why some don't change.

> We have much to say about this, but it is hard to explain because you are slow to learn. In fact, though by this time you ought to be teachers, you need someone to teach you the elementary truths of God's word all over again. You need milk, not solid food! Anyone who lives on milk, being still an infant, is not acquainted with the teaching about righteousness. But solid food is for the mature, who by constant use have trained themselves to distinguish good from evil. (Hebrews 5:11-14)

If we are slow in our character growth, it is our own fault. We can't blame our discipleship partners. Take charge of your life and constantly practice righteousness until you become mature. No person *can* do those things for you, and God *will* not. We want to be "zapped" into immediate easy change, but it does not work that way!

Other expectations can also damage our relationships. We can expect our discipler to have it all together. Only one Discipler is perfect and his name is Jesus. The human channels through which he disciples us are certainly imperfect and sinful creatures, although they are striving to be righteous. All humans have flaws. Even my angelic wife has some *minor* flaws—minor compared to her husband's! What would happen if I always focused on those flaws? Soon I would see nothing else! The same principle is true in all other relationships, including those with discipling partners. Deal with your own flaws, and let your love for your discipleship buddy cover over a multitude of sins (1 Peter 4:8).

Another unreasonable expectation can be looking for too much time and attention from those who already have packed lives. We have to practice the Golden Rule and not make demands of others that we would have great difficulty meeting were we in their shoes. Be full of grace and be appreciative, not demanding and disappointed.

There are other unrealistic expectations to deal with in discipling relationships, but these should help us develop a feel for what works and what does not. We cannot be spoiled spiritual children who are never satisfied because our expectations are too high. We need to concentrate on being givers who bring joy into the lives of our disciplers.

Value Accountability

As mentioned in an earlier chapter, accountability is designed only to help us follow through with what we are already committed to doing. It should never be viewed as added pressure to make us do what we don't want to do. I want to have quiet times with God daily, share my faith daily and do many spiritual activities consistently. I appreciate my brothers and sisters in Christ asking me how I am doing in these areas. Even at the age of fifty-eight, as a mature person who wears many hats of leadership, I need accountability—and I always will.

Once, in a discipleship time with Randy McKean, the two of us talked for a long while about personal discipline, specifically about the area of food intake. He has been dieting and has lost significant weight. His example convicted and motivated me to make a decision to imitate him. I committed to begin a new approach the next day and shared with him my weak areas in controlling my eating, requesting that he ask me about how I am doing in those areas. He agreed, but had me agree to provide him with a specific plan for losing the weight. When we met the next week I gave him a computerized chart showing my exact target weights for the next twelve weeks. Making myself accountable to Randy is no burden. Even if he had brought up the subject originally, I would still be appreciative. I need to lose the weight and I need help in doing it.

Our view of accountability reflects our view of demands and commands generally. One person looks at the sign which says, "Keep Off the Grass," and he is grateful that someone is trying to preserve the beauty of that environment. Another person looks at the same sign and feels a strong urge to stomp on the grass. It is a question of heart and focus.

Our view of accountability, whether from God's expressed principles or those we formulate to carry them out, reveals our hearts and our true motivations. If you do not see the value of accountability, you have a spiritual problem, period. Repent and learn to embrace every form of help available to promote your growth, *especially* accountability through those God has put in your life!

Schedule for Success

It takes time and scheduling to develop great discipling relationships. Jesus called his disciples to be with him (Mark 3:14). Daily contact is more than a good idea—it is in the Bible (Hebrews 3:13). We are out and about in the sinful world all day, which takes courage *out* of us. Thus, we need a brother or sister to put courage back *in* (encourage) us daily! The length of our phone conversations or visits will vary depending on the needs we have and the time we have available, but the contact itself is a blessing from God. Besides the daily contact, a weekly discipleship time is a reasonable expectation for all of us. Just to maintain our spiritual equilibrium, these weekly and daily settings are vital; without them the opportunity for growth is severely limited.

Not only do we need to schedule a discipleship time together, we also need to have a format to gain the most from it. Such times should include at least several things from the following possibilities:

- Sharing victories, struggles, sins, dreams, plans and anything else on our hearts about our lives.
- Opening the Bible for insights and answers to the above needs. I have a friend who has concluded that we need to begin every discipling time by reading a significantly long passage of Scripture so the word of God is at the heart of our time together.
- Sharing about exciting quiet times.
- Praying together—a constant. Discipleship partners should always be prayer partners.
- Asking advice in many areas. (Proverbs 12:15 states, "The way of a fool seems right to him, but a wise man listens to advice.")
- Obtaining input and direction for the upcoming week in our mission for Christ (and in related areas).
- Getting advice and direction regarding those you are discipling.
- Asking for loving accountability about the directions we received the past week (Luke 9:10).
- Going out to share our faith and serve others who need help.

Other good things could be added to the list, but the main emphasis is that the times should be scheduled, consistent, planned and spiritual. As I have already said, play and recreation should be a part of our friendships; however, if all we do is shoot hoops, watch sports or catch movies together, we will not help each other to grow continually stronger.

The practicals of discipleship will unquestionably work in your life if you appreciate the need for organization, think in terms of friendship, keep your expectations reasonable, value accountability and schedule for success. Be a disciple, be discipled and be happy!

part three

BEING A DISCIPLER FOR JESUS

chapter eight

BE A RELATIONSHIP BUILDER

As you mature in your faith, most of you will become responsible for discipling another person. This is a weighty responsibility and a precious opportunity, and the remaining chapters of this book will be devoted to this subject. Fundamentally, being a discipler means being a spiritual friend, and in most cases, an older brother or sister spiritually. I once heard the chain of discipling relationships in the church described something like this: as we are trying to grow in Christ, we reach up to join hands with someone who is more mature spiritually than we are and who can pull us higher; as we are being helped to grow, we then reach down to someone somewhat less mature spiritually than we are and pull them higher; Jesus is at the top of this discipling chain reeling us all in! This little illustration helps us to see how all of us fit in to the process of discipling as we help each grow and mature. Of course, sometimes discipleship partners may be on the same plane of maturity and would relate more equally to one another. But even then, you still have a spiritual buddy to help you grow.

If you are the discipler and the more mature person in the relationship, your leadership must be spiritual. The most important distinction between worldly leadership and spiritual leadership concerns the issue of relationship. Leaders in the kingdom are "servant leaders" (Matthew 20:25-28), not "bosses," at every level, and especially in the leadership exercised as a discipler. I cannot say this strongly enough. Jesus was emphatic on this point. All of our influence with a discipleship partner should be through the relationship (i.e. friendship) itself, not through a "positional authority" mind-set.

Generally, there are three kinds of authority found in relationships: *relational* authority, exerted by a trusted friend; *knowledge* authority, such as that of a doctor or other expert; *positional* authority, such as the boss with an employee. Discipling is characterized by relational authority and knowledge authority almost entirely. Thus, the person being discipled should have a humble and submissive spirit, but so should the discipler.

The apostle Paul was a master at leading others through relationships, and this truth is perhaps illustrated best in his interaction with the very young church at Thessalonica. Tremendous lessons may be gleaned from 1 Thessalonians in studying how he worked through relationships to keep those disciples strong and growing, even though he had only been with them physically for about three weeks. If we put into practice the principles found in this short letter, our relational skills will soar and our discipling relationships will yield blessings beyond our imagination. Let's search for Paul's relationship building "gems" as we strive to imitate his heart and effectiveness. (Important: the impact here will be much greater if you keep your Bible open to 1 Thessalonians and read each passage before reading my comments about it.)

Start a Smile and Compliment Club (1:2-9)

As you read this passage, you should be impressed with Paul's expressions of appreciation both for the relationship he enjoyed with the Thessalonian disciples and for their hard work. His gratitude for them was continual and his encouraging comments about them surely made them feel like they were very special to Paul and to God. Paul was a charter member of the "Smile and Compliment Club." Are you? He went on to challenge them in a number of ways, but the foundation he used for those challenges was positive reinforcement. It is often said that we need to hear ten positives about ourselves in order to handle one negative. A good friend and discipler figures out what helps us to keep our emotional and spiritual equilibrium and tries to meet those needs.

Obviously, we need to call others continually higher, but the issue is how to do that while helping them to build a good self-image and security in the relationship. Paul made his brothers and sisters feel like they were awesome in his sight and in God's. Then when the challenges came, they were fired-up to meet them.

Explain Your Motives (2:1-6a)

Paul neither demanded trust nor assumed it—he *built* it! The principal way he built trust was by explaining his motives. Some people seem to have a knack for making others feel uncomfortable in conversations. They tend to ask questions and make comments in a way that puts others on the spot or leaves them feeling apprehensive, wondering where the conversation is leading. We often make people ill at ease by not adequately explaining to them what our goals are.

None of us likes having the feeling that another person in a conversation with us has a hidden agenda. We appreciate someone telling us up front what they have in mind, then working through the discussion and ending by evaluating how well they think we covered the intended agenda. This business of being up front and open in conversing is terribly important.

Love As a Mother (2:6b-9)

Paul was a good imitator of Jesus, who possessed the positive qualities normally identified as masculine and as feminine. Jesus was the perfect human, and as such, he embodied every positive quality of humanity. Paul's love for people made him a good "mom" and a good "dad," as we will discover in chapter 2 of 1 Thessalonians. To begin with, notice how he described himself as showing a mother's love.

First, Paul was gentle. Picture a mother holding her newborn baby—talk about gentle and unintimidating! If you recall, gentleness is one of the Spirit's fruits

(Galatians 5:23). I can remember a time when I was afraid others would think I was not "hard line" in my leadership. Thankfully, I figured out that being "hard line" has much more to do with directness in speech than with demeanor. Speaking the truth in love (Ephesians 4:15) is all about honesty, not about decibels or facial expressions. Some of the most heart-piercing challenges I have ever received have been delivered in the most gentle fashion. Occasionally, I have needed to receive a challenge with a stronger delivery style, but usually, the right content alone will open my heart to hearing and heeding needed changes. (I am talking here about more personal times with others. When preaching, there is certainly the time and place for speaking with "a loud voice." See Jesus' example in John 7:37.)

Second, Paul was "delighted" to share not only the message but his life. This is truly a mother's heart. This is real family. Just how well do the people you disciple know you? The answer: only as well as you help them to know you! The need for openness in relationships cannot be overstated. Close spiritual relationships cannot be built without it. When I begin discipling a person, I want to find out all about their lives, and I want them to know everything about mine. I love taking long walks with a new spiritual friend and sharing all about our early years, our dreams and fears, our successes and failures—everything that makes us who we are. Bonding with one another in such ways knits our hearts and prepares me to really help the other person.

I believe one of the most important things I do with others is share my personal example. My adage is, "Never waste an experience, even a sinful one." When helping others work through their problems, I can nearly always find something from my own life with which they can identify. If I succeeded in a situation, they are encouraged by my example of success. If I failed in a situation, they are encouraged by my perseverance and repentance. Be like Paul; then those in your life will be drawn to your genuineness, and your subsequent relationship will build a security in them with both you and with God.

Third, he worked "night and day" in order to benefit them most. I remember many a night when Theresa willingly sacrificed sleep to care for our children when they were sick. I have discovered that losing sleep or otherwise being inconvenienced for someone has a profound effect on them. Are you willing to sacrifice in loving a spiritual brother or sister? Are you willing to really work hard and, with joy, to serve them?

Yes, Paul was a loving "mom," pouring out his life for his children. Mothers are not driven by duty, but by desire; not by their personal need, but by their children's; not by a seeking of recognition and approval, but by a longing to bless and serve those whom they love. Love those you disciple with a mother's love.

Love As a Father (2:10-12)

Paul understood that first and foremost a father must be an example to those he leads. Unless we, as spiritual leaders and disciplers, are truly righteous, we have neither the right nor the power to lead. The importance of being stellar examples to those whom we lead cannot be overstated.

One of discipling's scariest principles is that those whom we lead tend to dilute our strengths and intensify our weaknesses. This means that our disciples will not often rise above our strengths, but will surpass our weaknesses. In one way, the principle makes sense, because we are the leaders and should be setting the pace and the example for those who follow. In another way, it is a sobering thought and should motivate us to minimize our weaknesses and to further increase our strengths. None of us is perfect, nor will we be this side of eternity. But are we *trying* to be?

Paul goes on to show what qualities we need to be fatherly. Note the words Paul uses: "...as a father deals with his own children, encouraging, comforting and urging you to live lives worthy of God...." Fathers are the bottom-line sort of people who do not let sentimentality overrule reality! Mothers often are too governed by their emotional attachments, which is why God planned for babies to have both fathers and mothers. Yet, Paul's example is that all of us, regardless of our gender, are to be completely loving.

Close emotional attachment and challenge must go together if we are to elicit the most profound growth in those whom we disciple or otherwise lead. If fathers are only known as disciplinarians to their children, the children's view of authority, including God's authority, will be warped. If disciplers are known only for their urging, and not their encouraging and comforting, those whom they disciple will definitely suffer ill effects. Be a good mother and be a good father. Paul was; imitate him as he imitated Jesus.

Feel What They Feel (2:14; 3:2-5)

It is true that a sentimental leader is not very helpful in the long run, but neither is an unsympathetic one. We must learn to feel *with* other people, especially the ones we are most responsible for helping to grow. Trying to motivate those who do not think you really understand their struggles is a difficult task indeed. Sometimes "hard liners" think that recognizing the pain of others encourages them to wallow in their misery. Undoubtedly, this can be true with some people and they need to be discipled about their tendency. But just because someone might abuse the situation does not change what humans need from one another, and it certainly doesn't change what the Bible teaches.

There are several words in the Greek New Testament that can be translated "compassion." One is a long word (*splagchnizomai*) that is used only of God and Jesus. The literal meaning conveys the idea of being so carried away with another's pain that your heart feels like it is being drawn out of your body toward him. Read the following passages with that definition in mind: Matthew 9:36, 14:14, 15:32, 18:27 and 20:34. If you are one of those afraid of being too sympathetic or too feelings-oriented, you need a dose of Jesus! Surely you don't think that he felt his whole body drawn into feeling the pain of others without ever expressing it to them.

When someone is hurting, they need to talk it out. Once they are able to let the pain out, then they will be in a position to hear and accept the needed direction to deal with what is causing the pain. Failing to listen sympathetically is failing to love. But after we do listen, we must be sensitive in giving direction. Telling someone, "You shouldn't feel that way," is insensitive at best and devastating at worst! As disciplers, we need to learn to view their situation from God's perspective, combined with the love we offer them by feeling their pain. Don't be afraid to love, to listen and to direct your friend back to Biblical thinking. Just keep it all in the proper order as you do it.

Insist on Righteousness (4:1-8)

Paul expected righteous living. As we must often do today, he dealt with the area of sexuality and sexual temptations. We live in a wicked, immoral world, and none of us is immune to its influence on our thinking. Pornography has long been a temptation, but it has never been more available and accessible than today.

I ask those whom I disciple the hard questions about their personal righteousness, including (and perhaps *especially*) their sexuality. Lust and masturbation are often some of the greatest temptations men face, and many women struggle with them as well. If we are going to deal with Satan effectively, no subject should be off-limits between discipleship partners. This kind of openness necessitates that discipling relationships be of the same gender. Paul did not think any subject taboo or otherwise off-limits. Of course, dozens of other temptations and sins beside sexual ones need to be dealt with openly and frankly as well. If we value relationships as much as he did, we must also address issues frankly. Expect personal righteousness of those whom you love just as God does.

Teach Them to Love Each Other (4:9-10)

Since Jesus taught that love between disciples is the primary badge demonstrating to the world that we are his, we must all constantly teach others how to love more and more. Paul did precisely that in this passage. He commended them for loving, but urged them to practice it in increasing measure. The world understands the concept of the friendship (*philia*) type of love, but knows little of God's kind (*agape*). The first is often based on common interests, the latter is an unconditional commitment. Although the Bible is full of teachings about how to love, certain texts stand out (for example, 1 Corinthians 13:4-8) and should be studied deeply and applied often in our discipling relationships.

Don't Forget Eternity (4:13-5:11)

I am very thankful to be part of a fellowship in which the everyday life of a disciple is dealt with consistently. It has been said that some religious people are so heavenly minded that they are no earthly good! This is certainly an extreme, to be sure. But I think we often go to the other extreme. We do not think enough about the next life in order to keep our perspective about this one. I love being a disciple. Every day can be an adventure when we spend it hand in hand with God, doing his bidding. But some days are not like that for me, and assuming you are human, not for you either. A popular bumper sticker says, "Life is tough and then you die." Even in that cynical comment, there's truth to be found.

Paul, in his vulnerable way, said that he, at points, despaired even of life (2 Corinthians 1:8). In Romans 8:22-25, he wrote that disciples "groan inwardly" in this life. Life on earth, at its best, is still not heaven. And God never intended that all of our deepest longings be met here, even in the church! Heaven beckons, and we will never find our ultimate fulfillment until we enter its gates. When I read passages outlining Paul's suffering and mistreatment, such as 2 Corinthians 11:23-29, I find myself wondering how he stayed faithful in the battle. Not to wonder—he told us earlier in the same book:

> Therefore we do not lose heart. Though outwardly we are wasting away, yet inwardly we are being renewed day by day. For our light and momentary troubles are achieving for us an eternal glory that far outweighs them all. So we fix our eyes not on what is seen, but on what is unseen. For what is seen is temporary, but what is unseen is eternal. (2 Corinthians 4:16-18)

Paul was enabled to endure all that he suffered by keeping his focus on the next life. The issues of this life are sometimes extremely burdensome, and the only way to deal with those issues and those difficult times is to keep an eternal perspective. We need to help those we disciple to hold on to this perspective.

Deal Constantly with the Heart (5:12-28)

My biggest mistake as a young parent was in dealing much more with behavior than attitudes. It is easier and quicker to follow that approach, and it seems to work in the early years of children's lives. However, it is not really working, for all behavior must spring from the heart, and thus all work to effect behavioral change must be an "inside-out" job. The Jews whom Jesus confronted in the first century looked religiously great on the outside, but inwardly were full of "dead men's bones and everything unclean" (Matthew 23:27). Discipling of behavior must be done by first discipling the heart, which then will change the behavior. This is a time-consuming and energy-draining process, but all short-cuts will lead to horrible spiritual maladies.

In verse 14 Paul helps us see that not everyone we disciple needs the same things. "Different strokes for different folks" is a wise saying. As Paul puts it, "Warn those who are idle, encourage the timid, help the weak, be patient with everyone." What is good for the idle, may crush the timid. While the timid may need support, the weak may need direction.[1]

One attitude Paul dealt with in this passage concerned the Thessalonians' need to appreciate their leaders. It is misplaced humility for a leader to shy away from

[1] Some years ago, I heard my friend Joe Woods draw a helpful distinction between the weak and the uncommitted. Some of Joe's thoughts on this can be found, along with other useful material, in *The Disciple's Handbook* (Woburn, Mass.: DPI, 1997).

teaching on this subject. The very nature of leadership means that we are the very ones who must teach such appreciation. If we are teaching it in order to direct appreciation toward ourselves, we have a problem. But if we stress the honor of being servant leaders in God's kingdom, everyone will end up blessed—including us. Since Satan is always seeking to erode trust in leaders, we would do well indeed to fill our conversations with the names of leaders and the respect and appreciation we have for them.

The concluding part of 1 Thessalonians contains three of my favorite verses about attitudes. These three succinct commands in 5:16-18, if followed seriously, would change any person's life overnight! He simply writes:

> Be joyful always; pray continually; give thanks
> in all circumstances, for this is God's will for
> you in Christ Jesus.

Isn't this what discipleship is all about—helping your friend to be happy, prayerful and thankful in any and every situation? When we change hearts, we change lives. No blessing, other than salvation, could be greater than learning to think and feel like Jesus.

Discipling another person is not about shaping up someone else. It is about building a relationship that will inspire, motivate and guide. The practical relationship "gems" in this brief letter will change your life and that of your discipleship partner, as you learn from Paul, the "unlikely" relationship expert whose view of relationships was dramatically changed by Jesus.

chapter nine

BE A PATIENT TRAINER

People who are past their childhood years have characters that are well established, for good or bad. Changing them into the image of Christ will take time and energy and will require the help of others. The effective discipler needs a number of qualities and attitudes, none more important than patience. The training process is neither quick nor easy, but the rewards of helping someone become spiritually mature are eternally satisfying.

Train Disciples to Think

We have much the same goal with our disciples that parents have with their children—teaching them to think correctly. In the case of discipling, we need to teach others to think spiritually. Occasionally I hear concerns expressed about the possibility of someone's mind being controlled by a discipler. Controlling another person's mind seems to me impossible, but I would not want to do that even if I thought I could. The goal of discipling is to teach another person to think for himself, and yet to think like Jesus. *He* does want to control our minds.

From God's perspective, our minds are going to be controlled either by him or by Satan. Those who think they are in control of their own minds are thoroughly deceived by the devil.

> The god of this age has blinded the minds of unbelievers, so that they cannot see the light of the gospel of the glory of Christ, who is the image of God. (2 Corinthians 4:4)

Paul spoke of the right kind of Biblical "mind-control" in a number of passages. In 2 Corinthians 10:5, he wrote: "We take captive every thought to make it obedient to Christ." In Romans 8:5-6, we read,

> Those who live according to the sinful nature have their minds set on what that nature desires; but those who live in accordance with the Spirit have their minds set on what the Spirit desires. The mind of sinful man is death, but the mind controlled by the spirit is life and peace.

A few chapters later, he added,

> Do not conform any longer to the pattern of this world, but be transformed by the renewing of your mind. Then you will be able to test and approve what God's will is—his good, pleasing and perfect will. (Romans 12:2)

Other applicable passages could be included, but the point is that we either learn to think spiritually and be controlled by God, or we continue with worldly thinking and are controlled by Satan. A good discipler helps us do the former.

However, learning how to think spiritually after we have been so thoroughly trained to think unspiritually is a challenge. It takes much time and much help to rewrite bad programming. As disciplers of those trying to learn the new way of Christ, we are going to have to exercise much patience. But if we are excited about Jesus and the spiritual realm, we will be excited to train others. Now that I have become computer literate, I love teaching my friends what I have learned. When they learn a new and helpful hardware or software solution, their faces light up. Their appreciative response lights up my heart. This is the mind-set to keep when discipling about weightier matters. We are sharing with friends the most exciting things in our lives. It is not coincidental that Jesus spoke of sharing his joy with his disciples in the same context in which he spoke of them being his friends because he had shared the Father's business with them (John 15:10-15). It all ties in together. Sharing the most important things in life yields close friendship and great joy!

Keep these principles in mind when those whom you disciple are struggling with learning to think spiritually. They will slip and fall and get back up over and over again. You have one of several choices when they are struggling. One, you can be impatient with them, which will result in shutting down their openness. Then they will not share the troubles plaguing their hearts and will likely go downhill from that point. Impatience does more damage than most of us realize. Two, you can get overly concerned and "heavy" in spirit, which also shuts them down. At an earlier time in my life, I allowed struggles in the life of someone I was trying to convert or disciple to put me in a somber mood. Being sober is good, because sin is real, but being somber helps no one. Three, obviously the best choice is to stay full of faith, which helps you to keep upbeat and lighthearted. Just think: God has chosen you to help change someone's destiny in both time and eternity. Keep perspective and stay joyful.

Train Righteously

Leading others in any capacity, including discipling, must be governed by righteousness. The Golden Rule is golden, and it must rule relationships in the kingdom. One of the most damaging aspects of poor leadership is harshness. I came to the conclusion long ago that God will not ultimately tolerate harshness at any level of leadership. I have seen leaders with the tendency to be harsh who repented and changed, and I have seen God deal very strongly with those who did not repent. But a word of caution is in order here. I have also heard the charge of harshness used by those trying to *avoid* the challenges to change given by a discipleship partner or other leader.

In our society, most churches and church leaders have been anything but directive in the lives of their members. Most preachers and other leaders have mastered the fine art of almost saying something! But this kind of wishy-washy, wimpy leadership is the stuff of which modern religion is made. Therefore, when people start attending services or become members of a true Biblical church, they are going to feel some pressure while being taught to "obey everything" that Jesus commanded (Matthew 28:20). If their hearts are set on becoming like Jesus, the pressure will be welcomed and very helpful. If their hearts are beginning to harden, they are going to react with resistance and will often cry, "Harshness!" Between the extremes of no direction and harsh direction lies the truth of how leaders are to lead. One extreme is no less sinful than the other, although we are inclined to think that harshness is worse. Lack of leadership is just as bad, especially when we see its ultimate consequences. Yet, harshness can never be excused. It is unloving and ungodly.

Another area in which leaders must remain righteous is in keeping confidences. Disciplers are going to know much about the ones they disciple, which is only right, but discretion in handling that knowledge is of paramount importance. For designated church leaders, confidentiality has potential legal implications. Laws are not only quite specific in this area; they are also quite varied from state to state. Such laws do apply to leaders within all types of organizations, whether religious or business. Therefore, the scope and purpose of our study is not such that we should or could deal with this topic from the standpoint of the legalities.

However, considering our Biblical responsibilities as individual disciples, some basic observations are certainly in order. Sharing something about one person with another person, whether the information falls into the area of confidentiality or not, should be done with care. A good place to begin is with a consideration of the Golden Rule—if the situation were reversed, would you want the same things said about you?

The Biblical admonitions which forbid gossip and slander clearly apply. In Proverbs 11:13 a "gossip" is defined as one who betrays a confidence. The intent of the one talking is not at issue in the passage—only the result is! In Ephesians 4:29, all unwholesome talk is forbidden and is then contrasted with talk which is helpful for building others up and for benefiting those who listen. In 1 Peter 2:1, every kind of slander is forbidden. If you are not sure if something is slander or not, assume that it has that potential and take the cautious route. Apply the Golden Rule and the principles of these two passages to help you decide.

If you are thinking about sharing details about another person's life in a potentially sensitive area without their knowledge, ask yourself the following questions:

1. Why am I thinking about sharing these things?
2. Will my sharing benefit the one about whom I am sharing?
3. Will my sharing benefit the one with whom I am sharing?
4. In the reverse situation, would I want the same things shared about me?

As we grow as Christians, we understand more about the grace and forgiveness of God, and are much less self-conscious about our weaknesses. I have often said that it is a great comfort to know that I could not be black-mailed in any way regarding my past, because I have been very open publicly about it. Since Satan works best in the dark (John 3:19-21), being open with our sins is a major way to keep him from controlling us. This is why James 5:16 ("confess your sins to one another") is in the Bible. Therefore, all of us as disciples need to cultivate openness about our own lives, and to eliminate the pride which produces self-consciousness. However, our openness about another person's life is a different issue and needs to be handled with the care discussed in the above section. When you do feel that a third party is needed to assist with a discipling situation of a more sensitive nature or when confidentiality has been specifically requested, you should get the permission of the person you are discipling before talking with another person. Even then it is sometimes best to describe the situation in generic terms without giving the person's name. Overall, most of us need to deepen our convictions and heighten our sensitivity in this area.

Once again, as in all other areas of life, one of the greatest guides for relationships is the one Jesus gave in Luke 6:31: "Do to others as you would have them do to you." As a discipler, train *in* righteousness by treating your discipling partner *with* righteousness.

Leave Room for God

When we do all that we can as a discipler to train patiently with a righteous approach, one need remains: Leave room for God, for this is the finest demonstration of godly patience. One of my favorite passages regarding the dynamics of relationships is found in 2 Timothy 2:23-26. Because of its importance to the subject of being a patient trainer, I will quote it and explain its principles carefully.

> Don't have anything to do with foolish and stupid arguments, because you know they produce quarrels. And the Lord's servant must not quarrel; instead, he must be kind to everyone, able to teach, not resentful. Those who oppose him he must gently instruct, in the hope that God will grant them repentance leading them to a knowledge of the truth, and that they will come to their senses and escape from the trap of the devil, who has taken them captive to do his will.

Arguments are nearly always foolish and stupid, and they lead to quarrels and wars. A patient trainer of others is the Lord's servant, and the Lord's servant must not quarrel. He must figure out how to disciple others without having an argumentative nature himself or being pulled in by someone who does. Arguments always shed much more heat than light. What is the antidote for these kinds of impatient interactions with our fellow disciples? A number of components must be included in the cure.

One, refuse to quarrel. It is forbidden, and therefore to do it is sin. Self-control is available to us as a part of the fruit of the Holy Spirit (Galatians 5:23). We have the choice of quarreling or not. Don't do it. Avoid this relationship-damaging sin.

Two, be kind, for kindness is also a part of the Spirit's fruit (Galatians 5:22). Kindness introduced into a potentially explosive situation does wonders. Note the words of Proverbs 25:21-22:

> If your enemy is hungry, give him food to eat;
> if he is thirsty, give him water to drink.
> In doing this, you will heap burning coals on
> his head,
> and the LORD will reward you.

If kind actions will melt an enemy in due time, we can expect kindness to melt an emotionally aroused disciple much quicker. Stay calm and be kind—to everyone. The "everyone" includes your mate, your relatives, your children and your disciples. Sometimes we are most impatient with those whom we love most. It is an issue of pride. We might be willing to take much time carefully reasoning with someone else, but with those who are closer emotionally, we can take it personally if they do not capitulate to our ideas immediately. In this case, we are being prideful, insensitive and unreasonable. Be gentle, and be gentle to everyone.

Three, keep teaching Biblical principles in a calm spirit. I can remember many occasions when I dismantled bombs by patiently pointing people to the words of Scripture and having them read it for themselves. If we simply refer to it or state the principle in it or even quote it, they may still remain irate. However, when they read it aloud themselves, something happens. We leave room for God, and he works. Keep the Bible open and keep teaching.

Four, we must not become resentful. What does that mean in this context? It means that we avoid taking the words of the one opposing us in too personal a way. If they are saying untrue things about us or saying them in a bad manner, they are out of control, not us. Don't take it personally; it's really their problem unless you make it yours. Admittedly, great self-control is needed when being verbally attacked by another, especially someone emotionally close to you. But by God's Spirit, self-control is available for the asking.

You are God's gentle tool to guide others to repentance. You cannot make anyone do anything. Even God is not going to force them, so why should you try? Calmly and gently instruct with Biblical principles, leaving room for God.

Communication in discipling is highly important, and we must learn to follow the above principles if we are to communicate effectively. In a practical sense, I often describe the communication process as having three "gears." Gear one is the nice conversational tone in which we talk much of the time, which is neither very direct nor confrontational. Gear three is very confrontational, but is mostly misused. We stay in gear one as conflict avoiders until we cannot hold it in any longer, and then we shift to gear three and blow up and blow people away! In the kingdom, we need to function most of the time in gear two—that mode of directness and honesty which addresses the issues straight on in a calm, reasonable manner.

Patience is a virtue whose value is at its height when exercised to help another person become more like Jesus. Train patiently, train righteously and train without any hint of an argumentative spirit. In essence, just think of how physical children best respond to training and use a very similar approach in training spiritual children. Do your best, pray about the rest, and above all, leave room for God to mold the heart by using you as his tool.

chapter ten

BE A HUMBLE ADVISOR

One of the greatest blessings in the kingdom is being able to obtain good Biblical counsel, and as a discipler, to provide it for others. The Scriptures contain an abundance of wisdom to guide us in this vital area. However, because we are dealing with the crucial issues in people's lives and not all matters are clear cut, giving Biblical advice requires great care.

The Nature of Biblical Advice

Just how do we determine what advice should be given in areas involving application of Biblical principles? The Bible gives us the principles we need to live a life pleasing to God (2 Timothy 3:16-17, 2 Peter 1:3-4). However, it doesn't give us all details we might wish to know. In many cases, God states some things in very direct terms, which we call *explicit* teaching. In some cases, a Biblical teaching is *implicit*, in that a certain truth is implied but not expressly stated. The degree of certainty we can have about implicit teachings can vary. Some things are very clearly implied. Others may tend toward the "opinion" area we will look at more closely at the end of this chapter. Establishing guidelines for Christian conduct often is rightly done by using Biblical implications, but we need to be sure these are the ones about which we can have great certainty.

For example, what do you think the Bible has to say about a Christian marrying a non-Christian? It does not explicitly address the issue, but the implications are quite compelling. In 2 Corinthians 6:14-16, we find that we should not be "unequally yoked together" with unbelievers. The yoke here is not specifically applied to marriage, but no yoke in life has more far-reaching consequences than marriage. In 1 Corinthians 9:5, Paul argued that he had the right to take a "believing wife" along with him, just as did Peter, the Lord's brothers and the rest of the apostles. Then 1 Corinthians 7:39 says that a widow is free to remarry "anyone she wishes, but he must belong to the Lord." When you deal with a number of verses that relate to a given subject, the evidence can become very compelling in a certain direction. I have no question that the issue of Christians marrying only Christians falls into this category. Out of such implied, but definite, teaching comes further applications to dating practices of single disciples.

When we are working with implicit teaching, the further an issue takes us away from a clear Biblical principle, the more room for differences there will be. However, the important thing may not be so much the actual decision made or the actual advice given, but the attitude that we have through the whole process. Once again our point is: God blesses humility.

Our giving of Biblical advice often is no more than simply sharing a passage that directly addresses the issue under consideration. At other times, we are dealing with implications, which are derived by looking at a number of passages that relate directly or by principle to the topic of concern. Sometimes we may be looking at areas involving only judgment, which is based solely on experiences of disciples and what seems to have worked best. Regardless of which route we are following to determine the advice, we are seeking only what is going to bless the one whom we are advising. It may involve a choice of right or wrong or it may involve choices of good, better and best. In all cases, we need to remain Biblically grounded, practical and humble in advice giving.

Sometimes people get the idea that seeking advice means asking for permission. If that is the way those you disciple think, you should help them correct their view. A discipler is not someone who gives another disciple permission to do anything. A discipler is one who offers counsel based on his or her knowledge of the Scriptures, the people involved and the circumstances. It is up to the disciple to consider the input, be prayerful and make a decision out of his or her own convictions. Those who think in terms of getting permission not only view the situation wrongly, but they may tend to blame the advisor if things do not go well.

Faith or Opinion?

In giving advice, we must be able to distinguish whether we are dealing with an area of Biblical faith or an area of opinion. Unless the Scriptures clearly settle an issue, we must realize that advice is only advice, even though we are trying to base it on Biblical principles. The less specifically a topic is covered in the Bible, the more room for variations in its interpretation. Most of us would probably be more comfortable with all of the gray areas eliminated, leaving everyone in perfect agreement on every possible topic. However, God did not think that best—probably to make us less dogmatic and to keep us humble.

Thankfully, we do have many areas of black and white in the Bible. Sin lists, like those in 1 Corinthians 6:9-10, Galatians 5:19-21 and 2 Timothy 3:1-5 do not leave much room for variations in interpretation. Certain things are always right, and certain things are always wrong. None of us has to seek advice about whether to lie or steal, for these practices are categorically wrong. But many other avenues open to us are not directly addressed in the Bible, and decisions about them fall more into the realm of judgment or opinion. As those who advise others, we will quite often share our opinions and the spiritual reasoning behind them, but be compelled to leave room for alternate opinions. Raising doubts about the right or wrong of Biblically clear teaching is bad, but so is binding others by your opinions in areas where the Bible has not clearly taught the point in question.

Romans 14 is a key passage about the reality of gray areas, where the issues are truly matters of opinion and therefore viewed differently by different brothers. In Romans 14:1-8, Paul's point is that we have room in the kingdom for these kinds of differences. In such areas, we need to live by our own consciences and avoid dogmatism.

Specifically, he addresses the eating of certain foods and the observance of certain days. Jews and Gentiles had very different backgrounds and were comfortable with different practices in these areas. Without dealing with the specifics involved, since that is not our purpose, we can say that all of us are not going to have the same consciences in these opinion areas. Therefore, we had better be careful about binding our opinions as law. What seems perfectly clear to us may still be only an opinion.

In Romans 14:9-12, Paul makes the case that there simply is no room in the kingdom for judgmental attitudes toward one another. Narrow-mindedness and self-righteousness are condemned strongly by Jesus. We must keep our hearts knit together in spite of differences of opinion in certain areas and the tensions that may be thus aroused. When the Bible specifically teaches something, it is binding and must be followed. On the other hand, advice for individuals in areas of opinion is not in the same category. However, our attitudes must lead us strongly toward the seeking of agreement, not toward relishing differences—it is an issue of heart and unity.

Paul moves on in Romans 14:13-23 to argue against setting examples that destroy our brothers. We should not exercise our liberty in a way that causes a weaker brother to stumble. Nor should we ever violate our own consciences. Lest we interpret this section in a manner that contradicts the earlier sections of the chapter, note that causing a brother to "stumble" is equivalent to causing him to "fall" or "be destroyed." In my distant past when I was in a legalistic church, I often heard some argue that if a person did something that merely disturbed someone else, then the person should stop doing it. But the text doesn't say that you have to stop doing anything that might cause a cranky person to "grumble"—the word used is "stumble"! However, the point should be clear in reading Romans 14 that we have to maintain humility in giving advice and not bind or loose where God has not.

Seeking a Second Opinion

As disciplers giving advice, we need to know our limitations and learn to get plenty of collaborative advice. In other words, when giving advice, if you have any questions at all about what might be best, seek further advice from a mature spiritual person (keeping in mind what we have already said about confidentiality). The more significant the consequences of decisions being made, the more need to get this collaborative advice. As an elder of a very large church, I am asked to give much advice about very weighty issues. But, few actually seek more advice than I do, even when I have a good idea about the best route to follow. If the consequences of a decision are serious, I want to make doubly sure that the advice given is the best possible. Serendipitous in this case is the rapid growth in wisdom gained by seeking secondary advice. *A humble discipler or other leader at any level must be a serious seeker of advice himself.*

As one being discipled, we should be eager to seek advice and then to follow it. However, as mentioned in an earlier chapter, we cannot glibly follow it, especially if we have any qualms or questions of conscience. None of us should ever feel trapped as a disciple, nor should a discipler want to ever allow such a dynamic to evolve in a discipling relationship. Humility is required on both sides. Consider the following questions in being prepared to lead and follow in a spiritual manner:

- In giving advice and direction, is your approach to teach the other person how to think or to do their thinking for them?
- How can someone not follow advice without being independent and/or rebellious?
- What is your response when the advice you give is not followed?
- Are you comfortable letting someone you disciple know that you are open to bringing someone else in if they have trouble with your advice?
- What is the correct way to handle such an appeal as the one leading? As the one being led?

Your answers to these questions will tell you a great deal about your leadership, your followership and your heart—don't take them lightly!

What should be done when one being discipled cannot agree with the advice given by his discipler? No one should ever be, or even feel, boxed in. Our loyalty and allegiance is first and foremost to God. The right to get more input from another leader with more responsibility should be a component understood by both people in a discipling relationship.

Whether disciple or discipler, we are all works in progress. Perhaps you have seen the lapel button that reads "PBPGINFWMY!" ("Please be patient—God is not finished with me yet!") Be a humble disciple, and be a humble discipler. Clothe yourself with humility (Colossians 3:12), and you will be a well-dressed advisor to those whom you disciple.

chapter eleven

BE A GRACEFUL LEADER

One of the most precious aspects of God's nature is his strong urge to lavish grace on mankind (see Ephesians 1:7-8). Nothing motivates us better or longer than grace. When we really grasp what God is offering us, then we allow him to grasp our hearts and souls in a permanent way. My favorite book in the Bible is Romans because its main subject is grace. As has often been said, "If you get Romans, God gets you." When people leave God, I am convinced that something in their understanding of his graceful nature must be deficient. But if understanding and teaching grace is important, treating others with grace is more important. The means of motivating those under our leadership is absolutely a crucial issue, and we must be determined to motivate as God does. What are the keys to leading with godly motivation?

Acceptance

The foundation of our salvation is that God accepts us because of Christ, not because of our performance. Ephesians 2:8-9 says:

> For it is by grace you have been saved, through
> faith—and this not from yourselves, it is the

> gift of God—not by works, so that no one
> can boast.

Since man does have a part in his own salvation, in that he must choose it, we can develop an erroneous attitude about our part in the process. We are tempted to say that God's part *plus* man's part equals salvation. Stated another way, God's grace *plus* man's faith equals salvation. The problem here is the implication that our part is on an equal or near equal plane with God's part. A much more accurate way to describe the "grace through faith" salvation process is to say that faith *relying* on grace secures salvation. We, in no sense, earn redemption—we merely accept the work of God based on the cross of Christ. A spiritual song expresses it in this way: "He paid a debt he did not owe; I owed a debt I could not pay."

You may be wondering what all of this has to do with our discipling of other people. Actually, quite a lot if we are to lead and motivate like God does. He never says, "Measure up and I'll accept you." He accepts us in Christ and then works to help us live in a righteous manner. In fact, immediately after the verses quoted above, Ephesians 2:10 goes on to say,

> For we are God's workmanship, created in
> Christ Jesus to do good works, which God
> prepared in advance for us to do.

Works are a part of the plan, but we work because we *are* saved, not to *be* saved. Godly discipling follows the same principles, as we accept those whom we lead without putting them on the performance treadmill.

For the most part, we live in a world based on performance. Our neurotic society did not become such without cause. Even most of our families emphasized performance far more than they realized. Parents, even with good intentions, made us feel that their acceptance was conditional in many ways. They likely were trying to keep us reaching higher, but although this type of motivation might promote achievement, it also fosters insecurity. We simply must break the "perform to be accepted" mentality in all righteous relationships—between God and man, and between man and man.

My children are my children during all kinds of times, including the good, the bad and the ugly. In their growing-up years, I loved them when they were bad and when they were good. In fact, I probably felt more loving concern for them when they were not doing well. God is the same way as a father. Think of passages like Romans 5:8: "While we were still sinners, Christ died for us." When we are doing terribly, his heart reaches out to us incredibly. We simply must learn to treat one another in the same way, regardless of whether we are dealing with physical children or spiritual children. We can never emotionally shut someone out when they have disappointed us. Real friends stick with us through thick and thin.

We cannot resort to "doghouse" discipleship, by distancing ourselves emotionally from someone who has not measured up to our expectations. This approach to dealing with sin or disappointments in relationships is void of understanding the Biblical approach to resolving conflict in relationships. When wrongs have been committed, we are to call each other to repentance, not penance. The former focuses on God in seeking pardon, and the latter on self, in attempting to "work off" sins. The primary difference in godly and worldly sorrow (2 Corinthians 7:8-11) is whether we look up to God for help in changing or look down on ourselves in self-pity. Repentance produces a recognition of guilt and deals with it righteously by turning to God for both forgiveness and the strength to change. Penance produces a guilt trip and attempts to earn forgiveness in some fashion. Guilt is real, and its purpose is to produce godly sorrow; but guilt trips are satanic to the core. God has absolutely no desire for anyone to be put on a guilt trip.

We are all sinners, and as such, we are going to make mistakes—even though our goal is to not sin. Since God accepts us sinners in Christ, we are going to have to learn to accept ourselves and each other when we sin.

Freedom

The principle of accepting each other in Christ sets the atmosphere for enjoying freedom in our relationships. Many Bible-readers have marveled at how often the apostle Peter made mistakes. I marvel at the freedom Jesus gave him in which to make them! Righteous relationships are characterized by the freedom to be who we are while we become who we are meant to be. Read that sentence again, for much hangs in the balance here.

I once heard about a rather widespread survey of college students, in which their emotional stability and maturity were measured as a means of determining the effectiveness of parenting styles. The different parenting styles were distilled down into four basic types. One was the *authoritarian* style, in which the parents (usually the dad) ran the family like a drill sergeant. "Do what I say when I say it, and don't talk back." Another style was the *authoritative*, where the parents were definitely in charge as the leaders, but were not control freaks. A third style was the *permissive* and a fourth, the *indifferent*. The permissive parents allowed their children to mostly do just what they wanted, being afraid to lead more strongly. The indifferent were very uninvolved with their offspring, letting them go their own way almost entirely.

Which of the four styles do you think produced the most emotionally stable and mature young adults? The most effective leadership style was judged to be the authoritative, and the authoritarian was dead last. The authoritative parent loved enough to be involved and to set guidelines. The permissive parents were concerned but weak in leadership because of giving in too often. The indifferent parent had little or no relationship with his children, but the authoritarian parent had a bad relationship, and not surprisingly, one which produced by far the most rebellion. Therefore, parental effectiveness is tied to the quality of relationship between the parent and the child.

Jesus is unquestionably an authoritative leader. He is in charge, make no mistake about it, but he never tries to force us to do anything. This would be contrary to his purpose of developing a close relationship with us. He leads us, but he doesn't force us. He provides direction, advice and motivation, but he allows us the freedom to choose. We must do the same as we disciple others.

As disciplers, we are not simply trying to produce "a good Christian performance" in those we disciple. We are trying to set up the atmosphere of freedom, in which honesty and openness can flourish. Then a disciple learns to be more and more effective for God. If we do not make people feel free to be real, their hearts will not come out and therefore cannot be properly discipled.

Expectations

How do you tend to view people in general: positively or negatively? Your answer will tell you much about yourself. If you understand the nature of the world and its sin, you see the world as a messed-up place. As Paul said in Titus 3:3,

> At one time we too were foolish, disobedient, deceived and enslaved by all kinds of passions and pleasures. We lived in malice and envy, being hated and hating one another.

Hardly a pretty picture, is it? On the other hand, if you understand the kingdom of God and the righteousness he provides, you will feel quite another way about disciples. Paul also had a word to say about this side of the coin.

I myself am convinced, my brothers, that you yourselves are full of goodness, complete in knowledge and competent to instruct one another. (Romans 15:14)

Of what are *you* convinced about those in the kingdom—especially those whom you disciple? Your expectations of them will have an amazing influence on what they will become.

Have Expectations

In the first place, you must *have* expectations in the discipling relationship. Discipleship times are not simply cake and coffee times; they are times for discipling. Find out how your spiritual friend is doing in the most important areas of life. One way to cover these bases is to ask how they are doing in the four key areas of relationships: relationship with God; with family (if single, this includes relationships with roommates and with the opposite sex); with disciples; and with the world (evangelism and any problem relationships which might exist).

As you discuss these areas, focus on goals for each. Pick out what needs to be changed or done in each, write it down, and then share how things are progressing each week. If we have nothing to shoot at, we will hit the target with deadly accuracy, which means that we will be growing and changing very little.

What are the long range and short range goals for your life? What are they in the lives of those whom you disciple? Do you have expectations for yourself? For others? Goals and accountability are the stuff of which progress is made. Care enough to have expectations, to help others set goals, and then to hold them accountable for following through.

Have Reasonable Expectations

Our expectations in discipling should be reasonable in several ways. One, they should be individualized. We are all born with different capacities, and we have had different influences in our lives shaping those capacities. We have different needs and respond differently to events in our lives, to failures and to correction. Disciplers have to learn what each person he disciples needs and figure out what motivates him best. Some of us work well with certain types of people and don't have a clue about how to work with other types. The best leader is the one who can work with the most types of people. Study the example of Jesus on this point. Pay the price of learning how to disciple all kinds.

Having expectations which "stretch" our disciples is vital, but if we expect too much too soon, the faith of the people we are trying to help can be damaged, to say nothing of their self-esteem. Disciples really need to get advice before setting their hearts on their dreams, and we as disciplers need to be honest, yet sensitive, in advising them.

Two, our expectations need to be kept reasonable by seeking progress in disciples—not perfection—as our goal. This being true, we should be practicing what might be called "situational discipling," allowing others' life situations to determine when we will deal more heavily with character issues. In other words, we as disciplers should not constantly harp on deeper character weaknesses that will take a long time to change. Blatant sins of choice need immediate attention, but the deeper things are going to change more gradually. Keep in mind Doug Arthur's definition of discipling: "gentle pressure, relentlessly applied." Gentleness and perseverance are great partners in bringing about character change. Surely we all need to change our deeper weaknesses, but if that's all we hear about week after week in our discipling times, we will lose our love for discipleship. We need to deal with the deeply rooted character issues in our disciples as they manifest themselves in their life situations. Everyone will stay happier, and the growth will come in God's time.

Three, our expectations should keep us focused on training, not simply correcting. Our terminology at times indicates attitudes that are not the most helpful. For example, we may say after a strong correction or rebuke, "I really got discipled!" Well, if we needed a rebuke, praise God that we received it. But the way it was described leaves the impression that "getting discipled" applies only to strong, corrective direction, and it can cause younger disciples to fear both discipling in general and correction specifically.

Have Great Expectations

Yes, the expectations must be reasonable, but they must be nonetheless great. As you disciple others, express your faith in them. Just think of how Cephas must have felt when Jesus called him "Rocky!" (John 1:42)—and of how John must have felt to be invited into the Master's inner circle, even though he was almost certainly only a teenager. Jesus chose apostles who were the brunt of jokes and jeers as they formed the little ragtag group who followed him around. They looked common, they smelled common, and they acted common. But Jesus believed in them, and that was enough for them. His faith lifted them above the taunts and mockery that followed them all the days of their lives. And they became among the most influential men the world has ever known. The glory of the ordinary was that they became the extraordinary.

The apostles did not miss Jesus' point when they became the kingdom's leading disciplers. Paul took his Timothys, with their weak stomachs and timid personalities, and molded them into earth-shaking evangelists. Barnabas took Saul under his wing when the other apostles were all afraid of him and helped him change from a rabid radical into a minister of mercy. Barnabas stuck with John Mark, even when his weak character caused Paul to refuse to take him back on another missionary journey. The price tag for Barnabas was high in this case, for it cost him his position as Paul's right-hand partner in the mission field. You could clearly argue, as some have, that Paul made the better choice at the time, not letting sentimentality interfere with the mission at hand. However, I am more drawn to Barnabas than to Paul in this case! Paul grew to appreciate the man Mark eventually became, asking for him when in prison during his final days (2 Timothy 4:11).

Learning to be a graceful leader is a lifetime project, but the dividends paid will be far more valuable than almost any other adventure on which you could embark. Learn what these three words are all about: acceptance, freedom and expectation. Then on the Great Day when we all stand before God, many people in that vast throng will rise up and call you "blessed" for having given the kind of discipling that changed the course of their lives forevermore—praise God!

Who Are We?

Discipleship Publications International (DPI) began publishing in 1993. We are a nonprofit Christian publisher affiliated with the International Churches of Christ, committed to publishing and distributing materials that honor God, lift up Jesus Christ and show how his message practically applies to all areas of life. We have a deep conviction that no one changes life like Jesus and that the implementation of his teaching will revolutionize any life, any marriage, any family and any singles household.

Since our beginning, we have published more than 100 titles; plus, we have produced a number of important, spiritual audio products. More than one million volumes have been printed, and our works have been translated into more than a dozen languages—international is not just a part of our name! Our books are shipped regularly to every inhabited continent.

To see a more detailed description of our works, find us on the World Wide Web at www.dpibooks.org. You can order books by calling 1-888-DPI-BOOK twenty-four hours a day.

We appreciate the hundreds of comments we have received from readers. We would love to hear from you. Here are other ways to get in touch:

Mail: DPI, 2 Sterling Road, Billerica, MA 01862-2595
E-Mail: dpibooks@icoc.org

Find Us on the
World Wide Web

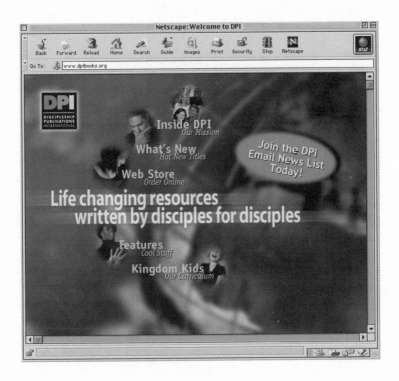

www.dpibooks.org
1-888-DPI-BOOK